The Prison Nurse

CH01086347

Before I fully start, I need to say that this is written as a true account and recollection of my experiences during my career as a prison nurse. I have not named any of the people in this book nor my colleagues to ensure confidentiality is maintained. The stories and accounts are true.

Why am I writing this book? Well, the answer to that is because so many people have asked me, 'what is it like working in a prison? Ooh that must be so scary. How do you do it? What made you do it?

So many questions and so much curiosity, I thought, this would be a great way to explain what is involved in prison nursing, and what being a prison nurse really entails. It would also give those who may be considering a career as a prison nurse some intuition. I want to try and explain what it is really like, what it was like for me and from my perspective.

Also, for those who nurse people in custody such as those being held in police station cells who require medical care and treatment for those working in immigration and detention centres. I thought it would provide an insight into prison nursing. These are not the normal routes that nurses take or even think about when starting their chosen nursing career. they are unique and not the most popular choices. Unless you have family or know someone who does work in a custodial setting or is being held in custody and carrying out a prison sentence, it is not something that crosses most people's minds.

I also couldn't find any books or information on other people's experiences when I was considering taking up the position and I had no previous knowledge of what it would really be like. I only knew of one girl I had previously worked with on a hospital ward who had left and gone on to become a prison nurse, so I contacted her to ask what she thought of it and for advice on what it was like. She basically said that you can easily become de-skilled, and that her main duties involved giving out medications all day. This did not exactly fill me with excitement, but I rang up anyway and requested a visit and asked if it would be possible to go in to have a look around and a chat before I actually applied for the job.

I actually ended up working there for thirteen and a half years, so I would say it definitely suited me and has been a major part of what I feel has been a successful career and an important part of my life.

Starting Out

When I was met at the gate and shown around, I will admit I was nervous. Who wouldn't be on their first time going into a prison? I mean people get nervous going through security in an airport or at a concert. It wasn't the first time I had been to a prison I had previously visited some friends when I was younger in a young offender's establishment and I had visited a friend of my sisters, but I only been into the visits hall previously although you still got searched.

Also, during my training as a student nurse, whilst working on the hospital wards, I met a male nurse who was working as an agency nurse on the same ward as me at the time and doing extra shifts. His primary employment was as a prison officer working in healthcare and had undertaken training to enable him to carry out healthcare duties the same as a healthcare assistant such as taking the observations of patients, administration of medications, taking bloods, dressings and such like. Anyway, he offered myself and some of the other nurses on the ward the opportunity to go into the prison with him supervising us and to show us around if we were interested. I had never thought about nurses working in a prison before, but agreed this was a rare opportunity that doesn't happen every day so agreed along with another girl to take him up on his offer.

He took us in and walked us around, he showed us the wings and the prison cells. This had been 14 years prior to the visit I had requested when interested in the vacancy because I was still a student nurse at that time, so it was a vague memory. I do remember that he opened a cell door told us to go in and I did first, then before the other girl could follow me, he pulled the cell door back and he locked me in! I felt very scared and thought, 'what's he done that for?' He didn't leave me in there for long, but I remembered it. He said, 'you never go into a cell without fixing the bolt first, because you can end up being taken hostage by a prisoner. 'I felt it was a bit unfair because I didn't have a clue about prisons, and I also wasn't an officer, neither did I have keys or had had any training in prison craft or security and would not have known any of those things. However, it obviously didn't put me off and I never did forget about that advice he gave me.

Upon arrival for my visit, I was met at the gate and shown around the healthcare unit and sat down and had a chat with the deputy manager of healthcare and I did not feel nervous being there. We were brought a cup of tea by one of the prisoners who worked in healthcare and offered toast. The manager walked me around the grounds, she was very friendly. What I noticed the most was the quiet at the time, there was no shouting or banging from the house blocks or wings as they are called, which surprised me. The prison grounds had beautiful, well-maintained gardens full of flowers and later a fishpond was built. It seemed to be calm and under control. I felt okay and thought then, that I would apply for the job and give it a go.

I really think this is so important to be given this opportunity to visit prior to applying but definitely before accepting a job because it does freak some people out and they feel very uncomfortable being in a prison and if you feel unsafe or anxious or uncomfortable and insecure, it is likely not for you and you should not feel bad about yourself, because it is not a weakness, we are all different and suited to different things.

I was definitely ready for a change in my career. I had worked in the same job and ward for the past thirteen years and felt ready to take on a new challenge in my life. My three children were all still in primary school but were settled and my husband, as always is supportive of me. I needed to progress to something new.

Firstly, the process after interview and then acceptance of the job offer is very long and slow. Do not be in the least bit surprised in waiting three to four months or sometimes longer before you are able to start your new employment.

I remember telling my friends and colleagues about my job offer, but after the initial excitement, and because the whole process takes so long, I began to wonder if it would ever happen.

You are advised not to hand in your notice at your current employment until you are officially offered a start date in writing. It takes a long time for the prison clearance and security checks to be carried out and depending on their Human Resources department, this can vary in time. If you have moved several times and changed addresses, banks or had financial difficulties these will all affect the process, because people in debt are deemed as being more vulnerable and could become the victim of manipulation from the prisoners, who may want to offer them payments for trafficking illicit items into the prison such as mobile phones, devices, drugs, or in this case pornographic materials.

It may take longer with the process of all the security checks when people have moved addresses frequently. They also have to look into family history for evidence of offenders or existing prisoners within the family unit because you could likely be refused a position if you could be influenced into illicit activities. You are certainly not employed if you have a previous criminal record or are held on any of the criminal registers. So, if you have had a stable address, and previous employment for a decent amount of time and have good credit record history, this will make the process go more quickly.

Usually the Disclosure and Barring Service (DBS) doesn't take too long.

I was employed for the first five years by the prison service and the Healthcare Department was under their control. After five years, the Healthcare Department was opened for tender, and the bid was won by an NHS trust. We were then TUPED over to the trust. This was excellent news for us, because as well as still continuing with the NHS pension, we continued on the Agenda for Change terms and conditions, which meant keeping our annual leave entitlements, pay bands and salary scales.

It also meant that we weren't completely controlled by the prison and were able to slowly devise our own policies and standard operating procedures to reflect our practice. We could now use paperwork and forms that were more relevant to our practices as some of the prison documentations were very archaic and were not current in keeping up with what we did in our everyday practice.

It meant we would be audited and scrutinised thoroughly by the Care Quality Commissioning body (CQC) to ensure our practices were in line with the National guidelines and that Clinical Governance framework was incorporated and adhered to. This would enhance and improve our performance and provision of quality of patient care to the service we provided.

It had a big impact on the prison staff especially the governors and heads of departments because some of them had been in their posts for many years and were used to controlling what we did. It sometimes meant they became very overpowering and demanding of us which as nurses we found it extremely difficult to push back sometimes and say no, we don't do it like that anymore and we need to follow the new NHS procedures which had made changes to what they had previously expecting us to do. We were used to carrying out requests from patients and doing what was asked, including by the staff but sometimes we had to become stronger and stand our ground, in order that we were following the correct procedures and practices.

There were many meetings to discuss and reorganise some of the existing forms used, attended by both prison staff and healthcare, because the prison wanted us to use their traditional forms for their documentation and records.

We ultimately were now required to use an NHS computerised healthcare system for documentation and were abandoning the prisons previous paper-based systems with an aim to becoming paperless.

An example of this was the F213 and the F213SH incident form. This was a form used by the Safer Custody department to record incidents which are used nationally for reporting and are used for national statistics. We had to complete and sign this when attending any incidents resulting in injuries, including self-harm, assaults and death. We would give a brief description of the event, and sign and date it. Even if we had not attended the incident at the time of the event, we were expected to go down to assess and examine the patient.

Most often these would be visits down to the segregation unit and were sometimes due to the patient having been under restraint. They were claiming to have sustained an injury caused from the officer's alleged use of force and were written in retrospect of the event. We would receive two versions of the event, the prisoners and the officers, as always, there are two sides to every story. The report we wrote had to be concise and factual and a record of the injuries and treatment given.

When we moved over to the NHS trust, we had to consider confidentiality and therefore we stopped recording the presentation of the patient as medical records require the patient to give their full consent to allow for sharing of information. You can try and imagine having that sort of conversation with a riled up angry man who has been taken down to 'the block' under force and knows he will be staying there for some time in isolation and with no access to his cell or belongings and maybe without a TV. So, we changed our practices and would only write, 'seen by healthcare' and sign and date it. This did not sit well with the officers and at first the forms kept being returned to healthcare from the safer custody department for us to fill them in properly. We would send them back informing them, we had. In fact, we were not obligated to complete or sign them at all, because they were not an NHS document but a prison document, but we had to come to a compromise that worked for both parties as we didn't want to cause a problem for them or us.

Ultimately, we still worked in the prison establishment and had to comply with the prison rules and work together with the prison staff and at the end of the day we all needed each other, they needed us to care for the sick ones, keep others healthy and especially in emergencies. During the Covid-19 pandemic we vaccinated almost the whole prisoner population in the establishment which was approximately 1200 people.

Many things began to change and continued to change over the next thirteen years whilst I was there. Things will continue to change to enable development for the future. This is the nature of the NHS who continually strive to improve.

So, if you are considering a job in prison nursing, give the healthcare department a call and ask if you can go in to meet them and be shown around first. You will know whether you are cut out for it or not from the moment you walk through those gates and are subjected to the security procedure and rubbed down, have your bag inspected and the wand waved over you. You will know how it makes you feel when you walk through the grounds with prisoners around you.

Categories of Prisons

I need to explain the different categories of prisons for those of you who don't know. Prisons are categorised as Cat A, B, C and D. A has the highest level of security and is for those people who have committed the highest level of offences. In the United Kingdom, this is murder, manslaughter, forcible rape and aggravated assault. Some may have committed more than one murder and sometimes this may have been whilst already in custody, where they have murdered another inmate.

These prisons will have a prison within the prison and are housing people who cannot be trusted to mix freely with others and have to be held in a very controlled unit. They sometimes require prison dogs and a minimum of three officers to unlock them. I will talk about a six man unlock I witnessed later on.

As the category reduces from A being the highest to D the lowest, the security level drops. Category A, B and C are known as closed prisons and category D are called open prisons. The category A prisoners are further divided into standard risk, high risk and exceptional risk. This is based on their likelihood of escaping. A Cat prisoner were not generally allowed to walk freely between their wings. This included walking to and from education, the workshops where they went to work, the chapel, healthcare, the gym, the kitchens or to the visits hall. They had to be escorted by the officers around the prison.

In a B Cat prison, which holds those prisoners in a reduced security regime. They have more freedom and can walk unescorted across the grounds, but the walkways will have officers stationed at points alongside the route enabling them to line it. Fights would break out on a regular basis and generally daily when the young offenders were let off the wings. They would start fighting because they were from different gangs in London and the prison had housed them purposely on separate wings to avoid conflicts on the wing and to try and reduce the numbers of fights and violence that occurred. They couldn't always keep them separated and they would establish contact in other activities in the other departments. They would pre-plan the fights and prepare weapons they had made and sometimes they had managed to conceal these in the grounds, in the flower beds of the gardens along the route or in their places of work despite having searches conducted when leaving the wings or workplaces. They still managed to get them out.

B Cat prisons, also known as local prisons, are where most prisoners go initially straight from police custody cells, and they are held whilst awaiting a prison sentence and court hearing if they are not allowed out on bail. Also, those that have been sentenced to a category B prison sentence for their crime. Some will be transferred to other prisons of other categories depending on the crime and the sentence they receive. Others will be waiting for a space in a prison which is offering a suitable programme which they need to complete as part of their sentence to reduce the risk of reoffending and is in relation to their crime.

Some people are constant reoffenders and are only serving short sentences of a few weeks or months and never make it to the transfer date to another prison as they get released before the transfer can happen. These are usually for smaller petty crimes such as shoplifting and burglary and theft. They are not deemed to be a risk to the public and are safe to be released back into society. B Cat prisons are generally those situated in cities. Most of them, are very old buildings, some Victorian and are smaller in capacity than the much larger establishments such as the one I worked in which held approximately 1200 prisoners. They tend to be the traditional style build of a prison with 3 floors high known as landings. These are often shown on TV programmes and documentaries and are what most imagine all prisons are like.

A Cat C prison is much more relaxed and once let off the wings in the mornings, prisoners can walk unescorted to wherever they are assigned to go. On a daily basis, several will choose to go where they please and they can easily hide amongst the throngs of people moving and are not questioned as there are so many moving simultaneously around the prison to reach their destination. This is called free flow movement. They get caught out when they are late or turn up in the wrong place because they are not on the list of assigned people. There are no officers once leaving their wings until they reach their destinations. They were often appearing in healthcare when up to no good such as trying to obtain illicit medications or hiding in the waiting rooms because they didn't want to go to work.

All prisoners have association time where that can mix and mingle with others on the wings at set times, except those who are in the 'seg', or deemed as dangerous or at risk of harm if on an ACCT document or a constant watch.

Cat D is also known as an open prison where they can go outside of the establishment's confinements during the day to attend outside employment but must return at night. This is to enable them to integrate back into society to see how they will cope. They are usually transferred to a Cat D prison after having served many years of a long sentence. They need to learn how to cope in the outside world again. You have to bear in mind some of these people may have served many years of back-to-back sentences. I met one man who had served a triple life sentence which equated to 15 years consecutively. He had started his sentence at age 30 and was finally released at age 75 years. He had shot and killed police officers, and this was his sentence. Imagine how things have changed in society in 45 years. He would not have known ATM cash machines, certainly not mobile phones or computers, IT technology, electric cars or for him to even understand the value of money. We are now becoming a cashless economy system. It must be a minefield for someone that age to comprehend, even the TV and how to access all the channels we have available today and social media.

Having described the different categories as well as progression down the category levels as the security risk is reduced for good behaviour, over time and compliance with the systems and rules, the security risk would be reviewed. Prisoners could be 're-catted' or re-categorised to work towards their release date and move down the levels.

Similarly, when displaying bad behaviour, they could receive further sentencing and have to re attend court which could result in moving up a category of prison with a higher security level. This included instances of assault on other prisoners or on staff and for taking others hostage or causing riots within the prison. They would be moved to other prisons for instigating gangs of racism, radicalisation, paedophilia, religious cults and drug dealing when they were discovered. This was a way to separate the drug dealers and bullying if they were the ring gang leader.

The prison I worked in was a Cat C male prison housing sex offender. When I started there, they had recently expanded the site from housing approximately 720 prisoners to 1200 prisoners. They had just finished building a whole new prison adjacent to, but within the grounds and fencing of the original site. It was separated from the original site by fencing and gates. The new site was to accommodate 500 Cat B young offenders or 'YO's' as they were called.

The original site was solid, and brick built in the 1970s and the newer side was prefab and much less robust. It was built quickly to accommodate the expansion to house 480 young offenders. They all were housed in individual cells, as cat B prisoners and they needed to be as they could get violent and had a lot of energy and testosterone. these were 18- to 21-year-old males. A lot of whom were in London gangs and were used to fighting.

Neither of the sites could mix. They had built a duplicate of another establishment alongside which means there were two of everything. Two Healthcare centres, chapels, gyms, workshop, kitchens, education department, segregation units, the list goes on. The only way the YO's would transfer to the original site is if they reached age 21 and were still serving the sentence and it was for the same offences as the adult offenders and was appropriate with the correct programmes they needed to complete within their sentence.

When I started there were many new staff who had also been employed to accommodate the new expansion of the prison. Some were brand new inexperienced officers who were fresh straight out of their prison training. There were many other new officers who had been employed on deployed duty. Their main posts were in other establishments, but they had been brought in whilst others were waiting to be cleared by security for starting their permanent posts at the prison.

The prison security checks can take months to be completed as I previously mentioned.

I also had to sign the Official Secrets Act when I joined, to ensure you maintain confidentiality when you are employed by the Prison Service which is a government department. As a registered nurse you are classed as a public servant when you are employed by the National Health Service and although I was being employed by the prison service and working in the healthcare department, I was able to continue working under the same terms and conditions, on the Agenda for Change on the same pay scale as when working in the NHS. This was fantastic for me as I had already worked for the past thirteen and a half years and been paying into the NHS pension scheme. The terms and conditions I was entitled to were continued, which was to be of great benefit as I had worked continuous service in the NHS. This meant my annual leave entitlement was also carried over enabling me to have the maximum allowance for having worked over 10 years of service.

Previous Experience

So, what experience had I had previously? Was I going to cope without having any prior knowledge of prisons, the justice and custodial systems and settings? I had worked on a hospital ward for the past 13 years which was a Respiratory Support and Sleep Centre. This was far away from going into taking responsibility for the caring and treatment of 1200 adult men. Most in general were fit and well physically, and being cared for in a primary care setting, which was essentially similar to community care. The difference being they were confined to the four walls surrounding them, for sometimes long periods of the day and night. Their freedom of liberty had been restricted, whilst being confined and serving their sentences. Their cells had now become their 'own homes,' so to speak, but with the added supervision that the officers and staff provided.

That sounded simple enough, I thought on first appearance, but how different it was all going to be. There was so much to take on board and understand and to learn about caring for prisoners, who believe me, are a different kettle of fish to the general public. On top of that I had no clue about the prison regime, how things worked, the language, terms, acronyms and abbreviations used. The whole of the wider prison system, security, daily routine for the prisoners both on and off the wings. How did the healthcare department and we nurses fit into all of this? What were our duties and what were the restrictions on what we were and weren't allowed to do?

All of this was to be considered alongside maintaining the nurses Code of Conduct which is the Nursing and Midwifery Council's (NMC) rules you agree to abide by when becoming a qualified nurse and join the register. We pay an annual fee and have to prove every 3 years that we are practicing to the expected standards by a re validation process. We are responsible for keeping our own records of hours of practice, hours of study and courses we do to ensure we keep updated in our practice and are safe. We also now have to submit reflections of practice and feedback from patients to ensure we are providing a good safe considerate standard of care.

The NMC standards include confidentiality, empathy, caring, compassion, communication and respecting dignity, to name a few. It is structured around four principles which are, prioritise people, practice effectively, preserve safety and promote professionalism and trust.

Of course I had 13 years of nursing experience, so the practical care was not an issue for me, and neither was the administration of medications, or so I thought. The medication rounds in the hospital were very straightforward. In the hospital, all you had to do was follow the prescription charts, check the patients identification and give them the medication, simple. In the prison this proved to be nothing like simple. I will explain this later, how it worked and how it changed over the years that I worked there.

I had also never experienced working in an Accident and Emergency department except for two or three days during my training. Neither had I dealt with minor illnesses or injuries or having to cope with anything that 'walked through the door' so to speak and certainly not with any emergency situations, let alone the wounds caused by assaults, both to other prisoners and staff. We had to make decisions whether to send someone out to hospital for suspected fractures, and for emergencies such as aortic aneurysms with dissection (this is very rare, when the aorta, the main blood vessel from the heart, ruptures and can very quickly lead to death. It is caused by high blood pressure and requires immediate surgery to graft and repair the ruptured vessel. If left untreated or improperly treated, 90% of people will die). There were heart attacks, attempted suicides, diabetic ketoacidosis, which can result in a comatose patient, perforated bowels, overdoses, self-harm and self-mutilation to the extremes of butchering his own genitalia (more later).

I was so NOT prepared for what I was about to start as the next stage in my career, I was going in blind!

I had never known any family or friends that had worked in either prison or police services and had never previously contemplated prison nursing. It is not generally something that crosses your mind when you go into nursing as a career. I mean I was not a new young fresh nurse. I had had several other employments prior to even taking up nurse training. I had gained many life experiences and been travelling and back packing, so I was not totally naive to life, people and the world around me.

Previous employments which helped me develop my character and basis of experiences included the civil service where I was employed in the Unemployment Benefit Office and the Job Centre. I had worked in several offices, both in small towns and in London in a deprived area. So, I did have some in dealing with people with little money and prospects, with poor or no education and those who had substance and alcohol abuse and dependence and were living homeless and in poverty. This was back in the mid-eighties and sadly those numbers of people have increased tremendously since then. They could get very angry and abusive with frustration when they hadn't received their 'giro' cheque, (their payment of benefits).

I also worked for a few years as a sales representative/ delivery driver for a local auto electrics company which provided servicing, repairs and replacements of auto electrical parts and equipment to the automotive industry. This included car and commercial garages, marinas and agricultural businesses and sometimes individual farms. This was a 99% male orientated world, and I was used to dealing with male customers and their chat and banter, in a professional sense, I didn't mind that. So going into the prison environment was also a largely male environment, definitely the prisoners, but also the prison staff, but over the years this has changed and certainly at the prison I worked the female staff numbers have risen significantly, this includes mentioning we had two female governors.

After the sales rep job, and backpacking I got the taste for working abroad and managed to get a job working on a cruise ship. I mentioned earlier that the abbreviations and acronyms used were like talking another language. It felt like people were talking in riddles. This was not dissimilar to when I started in the hospital where again everything is abbreviated, and people talk in codes. You just have to learn what all of it means.

Comms

The main communication system used across the prison site was primarily radios, which is pretty standard across all establishments. I had to learn the phonetic alphabet. I attended the induction training which when I started was run by the prison staff. You received radio training and learnt how to sign on the radio when starting on duty and signing off at the end of your shift, and also in between if you were leaving the site during the day such as at lunchtime. We each had a call sign to identify which department you were. The healthcare call signs were all 'Hotel' call signs, the nurse holding Hotel 1, was the 'on call duty nurse' that day, although all the nurses carried them and had to be available for any emergency calls that were put through. We generally went in pairs if possible and if required.

These radio calls were put through on a regular basis and would be for anything from minor incidents and requests to visit someone on a wing who was feeling unwell to codes of 'code red' and 'code blue'. Code red, generally meant anything involving blood, assaults, injuries, accidents and code blue, generally meant involving breathing and included, chest pains, shortness of breath, unconsciousness, overdose, fitting and faints.

We had to respond and attend immediately, grabbing the nearest emergency first aid rucksack, the defibrillator and the oxygen cylinder and run to the incident. It was extremely heavy, the site was big, you can understand why we generally went in pairs, actually getting the equipment to the incident was a feat in itself, by the time you got there you felt like you needed the oxygen yourself.

We had to negotiate stairs, unlocking and locking gates and doors to reach the incident and going across the open yard and grounds. Which was a distance. This sometimes happened during free flow, so we also had to negotiate moving prisoners along the way. We should have had officers to assist us at the entrance to the wing or area we were attending, to assist in unlocking the gates and direct us. Usually we would arrive and have to do this ourselves and then arrive to find no one in sight because all the officers would be clustered around and outside the cell door of where the incident was, but we would be trying to locate them upon reaching the wing as there were many spurs and landings to find out where the action was. This took precious time and sometimes we had to request the exact location from comms, it did however mean we could at least catch our breath before steaming in.

The benefits of having radios meant all staff carrying a radio could reach others when needed and difficult to locate them because the officers on the wings were not stationed behind desks with telephones, we nurses were in clinic rooms or on the wings visiting patients, there were the officers who worked in the workshops, the gym, education etc who all may need assistance at any time. It also meant if you got into any trouble and were unable to get to a phone you had your radio. This had an emergency button on it which could be pressed to get help and assistance if you were, God forbid, taken hostage.

We had code words we were not allowed to use in the normal dialect because they were for emergency situations only and if used, the alarm would go and officers would race to assist, the prisoners would not know these words or that you were speaking to the radio, so you could hold the button down and incorporate them into the sentence and they should come to the rescue. Luckily, I was fortunate in that I never had to use them and neither did my colleagues.

The other alarm we used was the general alarm buttons which were in all areas of healthcare and around the whole prison, these would be pressed at any time of need by any staff if a prisoner was getting aggressive and aggravated and the staff were at risk of this escalating into an out of control situation. When pressed the comms would announce where the alarm was, and all officers would run to attend and assist to deescalate or use force if required to maintain the safety of the staff.

During my thirteen years of employment, there was only one hostage on a female prison officer and there were two incidents of prisoners taking other prisoners hostage. This was when we had the young offenders. The poor female officer was new on the job and inexperienced, she was taken into the prisoners cell and she actually passed out, I don't know whether this was through fright or he had her in a strangle hold but it was the other prisoners on the landing that alerted the officers to help and they were attempting to talk him down and release her. I did feel sorry for her and to give her credit she did actually return to work after the incident. She must had suffered with trauma from this event.

I had no chance of being taken hostage. We had a man who had been sent up to healthcare from the gym where he had cut his eyebrow as a result of being hit by a badminton racket during a game. I glued the wound on his eyebrow together but managed to get the rubber glove and my hand inside it stuck too. He joked about having to take me back to his cell, but my colleague told him, 'No mate, you won't want to be doing that, she talks to much, she'll chew your ear off, and you'll regret it and be begging to send her back! 'Charming,' I laughed, she was probably right. I did manage to get the glove off the wound, after 2 x attempts , I sent someone to the vending machine to get Coca-Cola which dissolves the glue but the first time they came back with diet coke which doesn't work, it needs the sugar content, so another can later and we were sorted.

Tap Man

We arrived at work on a Saturday morning. We'd just put the kettle on for our first cup of tea of the day before starting to prepare for the morning medication round, when the radio kicked into life, 'Can any member of the healthcare team attend Delta wing?' a voice asked. I groaned, 'oh no, what now? 'We were always being called as a matter of urgency for sometimes very trivial things, it seemed, and it always seemed to be when we were busy doing other important duties. The morning medication took a lot of preparation. More so on a weekend, because there were no pharmacy staff on duty and so the nurses were responsible for administering all of the supervised medication, 'see to take' to the whole prison, which was a large establishment. Any interruption that time of day was a pain to say the least! My colleague said "I'll go to D wing if you want? And check him over, if he is ok, we will send him out for a check-up if he needs it, that will leave you free to start the meds." "Are you sure?" I answered, "I don't mind going". "No, I'll go, you start the meds" she confirmed.

Another colleague and I busied ourselves by preparing the controlled drug medications for delivering to the prisoners on the wings and for those who would be attending healthcare. The officers who were sat outside the medication dispensary told us, "The nurse has just come back and gone again quickly with that big blue bag!" "oh," I answered "It must be more serious than we thought if they've come back for the emergency bag" we carried on with the meds preparation, then a few minutes later my colleague appeared looking flustered to tell me "I don't know what to do, he's done himself some serious damage, he needs to go out and they are refusing to send an ambulance". My colleague went down to the office to ring the wing for more information,

-If we don't know what we are attending we don't know what to take- it could be to take a look at someone that has self-harmed during the night or sometimes just to give information regarding someone who has been moved from his wing to the segregation unit (CSU) or anything not a priority but still interfering with what we are doing at that time of day.

She returned from the phone "Oh my god someone's gone and put a tap up their arse and isn't feeling very well now, doesn't know if he's done some damage to himself" "Bloody hell what's he done that for!" I replied, honestly you couldn't write it! Then I thought to myself but I'm going to write it. This is such a unique and bizarre place of work- you cannot make this stuff up!

So here goes... 'Apparently, they've called the ambulance twice now because they found him a while ago, when he pressed his cell call bell. When the officers described the incident to the ambulance service, they were told that they were not sending an ambulance in and that the Healthcare department could deal with it when they arrived at work,' my colleague relayed. I guess they got the story of 'we've got a prisoner who has shoved a tap up his arse and thinks he's done himself an injury,' when they answered yes to the automatic questions that he was conscious, breathing and speaking, the response was that they could send him to hospital in a taxi.

My poor colleague was very concerned, and I could tell from her face and voice that we needed to act quickly and that he was in a serious condition. I said, 'don't worry, you go back to look after him, do you want me to come? I will escalate this.' I rang the orderly office and very clearly stated, 'we need an ambulance, NOW, forget about the tap and what he's done, this man is rapidly going into shock and if he's not treated quickly, he could arrest and then he could die! If we don't get an ambulance now, we'll need a helicopter! Can you please ring them back? He needs to go out NOW'. This seemed to spur them into action, and they agreed. I said, 'tell the ambulance that he's grey, clammy and sweating, his blood pressure has increased but then it will drop, his pulse was fluctuating between 40 and 130 beats per minute, and he had a National Early Warning Score (NEWS) of 5.

The NEWS is a scoring method which is used to indicate how serious a patient's condition is, how frequently, observations should be undertaken and is used to assess the seriousness of the condition and determines when to send someone into secondary care i.e. the hospital setting, which in this case was urgent and we needed the additional support of paramedics and an ambulance with supplies that we did not stock in the prison healthcare such as intravenous fluids and medication to stabilise his condition to enable his transfer to the hospital.

He was sitting on the toilet in severe pain and was extremely scared. He had told my colleague, 'It's never done this before, it didn't feel like that last time' indicating that he had done this before. He said, 'I felt it go pop'. He was terribly embarrassed about what he had done, and it was not an appropriate time to begin questioning him as to why. We had to deal with the patient's condition and the current situation and act quickly. We were informed that an ambulance was on its way and thankfully it arrived shortly afterwards. My colleague not only had to deal with a rapidly deteriorating patient who was becoming critical, she also was fighting to get the ambulance service to respond. There were two incidents which arose from this, one was the actual incident of the lack of response of the ambulance service, which would require an investigation, and the second was the lack of privacy and dignity afforded to the patient.

The cells were in corridors, known as spurs, with 15 cells in each spur. When anything is happening, all of the prisoners can hear what is going on despite their cell doors being locked. We have to communicate through the radios to the communication centre, known as 'comms' and they are on a land line speaking to the ambulance control. If you are too busy attending to a patient, you then have to rely on speaking through an officer. There were several officers from the wing gathered outside the cell door in the corridor on the landing and several more senior officers arriving to find out what was happening in regard to arranging the transfer to hospital and organising the escorting officers. You can imagine lots of loud excited chatter about the incident which would have been overheard by all the other prisoners on the wing. The main question my colleague had to answer, she said was, 'No the tap is not still attached to him- she was asked this seven times, and also asked how far up him is the tap and where exactly is the tap located?' it seems they were far too concerned about the tap and not about current condition of the patient!

The patient's rationale as to why he had been performing the act was that he was trying to give himself an enema. He was actually doing it for gratification. He was very embarrassed and did not want any of his family to be contacted or informed that he was being sent to hospital.

It transpires he had indeed perforated his bowel right up to under his ribcage at the junction of the transverse and descending colon. He underwent major surgery that day and was sedated and ventilated. He had an abdominal lavage, and a colostomy was formed. He was treated with several intravenous antibiotics and intravenous fluids. He was made nil by mouth, had abdominal drains inserted and nasal-gastric feed and was fighting for his life. He was a very poorly man! He stayed in hospital for several weeks but did luckily make a full recovery and returned to the prison with a stoma. It was incredible as we all thought we had lost him. This is one of the many incidents that I can recall and will stick in my memory due to the type of injury. It is so obscure and hard to believe that someone would do such a thing.

Self-Harm

Self-harm is a common occurrence within the prison environment. Some of the more serious injuries are caused from deep rooted mental trauma that people have been subjected to themselves and usually from an early age which manifests and due to feelings of shame, guilt and lack of self-worth, loneliness, lack of love, self-punishment or hate that they have hurt others they internalise their feelings and actions to cause harm to themselves. There are some very psychologically damaged people living behind these walls.

Some of the acts of self-harm, like the incident just described are used as a form of self-gratification. We had another man who used a chair leg which he would back himself onto and insert into his rectum and another who used bottles and made rolled up tubes from newspapers with blades which he had inserted which caused him to shred the lining of his rectum. Once he inserted an orange, (fruit) into his rectum and had to go to Accident and Emergency to have it removed as he couldn't get it out.

Self-harm was inflicted regularly, normally by cutting themselves with razor blades, removed from the shavers, but could be made with plastic knives or cutlery. We were not allowed to eat our lunch with metal cutlery for this reason and all the staff rooms and the bistro did not have any metal cutlery in them. Any metal tools or knives in the main kitchens of the prison, even in our staff room, the tin opener, had to be kept on a shadow board in a locked cupboard. Tool checks were undertaken twice a day and signed off in all departments by the staff. I found it very strange when I started there that I was not allowed to carry scissors in my pocket, as a nurse, I had always had scissors to hand. They all had to be accounted for and were kept on chains attached to dressings or emergency bags or in the cupboards locked in the treatment rooms. Alongside this were metal tuning forks, laryngoscopes, and examination equipment. If the prisoners were issued with splints when they returned from hospital having sustained muscular skeletal injuries, they would have to be checked to see that they didn't contain any pieces of metal as it would be very easy to make them into weapons.

Some of the men were serving life or indeterminate prison sentences with no release date and they had a lot of time on their hands and were very ingenious. When I first started at the prison, there were 480 young offenders aged between 18-21 years old who had been sent in mainly from the London prison establishments and were serving sentences for gang related crimes. The prison was a lot more violent then with outbreaks of fighting occurring regularly, as much as daily or even several times a day. There were a lot of young men, with a lot of testosterone, angry, frustrated and bored. The weapons could be made by sharpening the end of a toothbrush handle to a fine point to be used in a stabbing and by putting razor blades into a toilet brush and used to lacerate and shred someone's skin into ribbons. They would regularly throw boiled sugar water into the face or onto another's skin, which would stick and cause terrible burns and scarring and would stick to the skin and was extremely painful.

I attended an incident one day where two ceramic mugs had been smashed simultaneously onto both sides of a man's head causing a head injury and horrific bruising and cuts. They were vicious!

During the time of the YO's, they started a riot on one wing whereby they managed to take control of the wing, they rampaged, turned the pool tables upside down, had the legs off it to use for weapons along with the pool cues. The Tornado team were called in with the dogs – lots of prison officers, kitted up in full riot gear wearing helmets shields, full body protection with vests and padding on their legs. Whilst waiting for this national team to arrive from all over the country, all the staff on the wing and 2 x nurses had to stay locked into the wing office.

When the team arrived, it was the dogs that the Young Offenders were more scared of than of the officers and as the tornado team went out onto the landings, they just grabbed bodies and threw them into cells working their way along the landings until they had managed to regain control. It didn't matter that they were in the wrong cells, but they were behind their doors and that was all that mattered. I must admit, I found it all very exciting and is probably why I have been in the job for so long, you never know what to expect and you can go into work thinking you have a planned day ahead of you with clinics booked and within seconds it can change when something urgent occurs and changes it all in an instant.

We also had 'jumpers' which were the prisoners who climbed over the railings on the wing and threatened to jump from the landings. There was netting on the induction wing between the landings as this building was 3 floors high and the netting prevented anyone falling a great distance. Over on the other side of the prison the landings on the wings were only two storeys and therefore they were not as high, and they did not have netting. It was mainly when we had the young offenders that we had the most threats of them jumping. We had to call the outside team in on a few occasions where they would bring in full-sized blow-up inflatable mattresses in order to break a fall. This took a long time to get them in and set it up. Usually by this time the offender had got bored or been talked down and climbed back over the railings. Each time this happened, healthcare were called and had to attend in case they actually fell and caused an injury.

I remember being called once on an evening shift with my colleague as there was a man who had climbed up onto one of the metal storage units which was beside the poly tunnels in the gardens where they grew vegetables. It was our break time, and we actually took our cups of tea over with us as we knew it could be some time that we would have to wait. He had climbed up there because he had ordered some vapes from the canteen. Canteen is the term used for the weekly delivery of items they were allowed to purchase from their account if they had credit available. They ordered them from a canteen sheet and the items were limited and included things like shampoo, deodorant, creams, chocolate and biscuits.

He was claiming the vapes had been stolen from him and he was protesting because he had been to speak to the officers and was saying that no one believed him. Of course by climbing up onto the unit and refusing to get down meant he was now in even more trouble and that he would likely be going to the segregation unit, which he knew and that's why he was now trying to barter with the officers saying that he would only get down if they promised he would be allowed his vapes. Of course, they did, because they wanted him down.

We had another similar incident that again involved a prisoner who had climbed up onto a metal container in another part of the prison grounds When he agreed to get down, he jumped and ended up injuring his ankle quite substantially.

After two and a half years, the prison went under a re-categorisation and all of the young offenders were transferred to other prisons and we were filled up with adult only offenders, all over the age of 21. This made the prison less violent. A large proportion of the population were older men. The oldest we have ever had so far, serving his first sentence, was aged 94! Some of them received sentences in their eighties and nineties for crimes committed several decades previously. I don't think this is always the best place for them to serve their sentences.

I understand that the victims need justice and have suffered mental trauma for years and some have suffered silently not daring to admit they had been abused. However, some of the men have started to or already have developed dementia and cannot understand where they are or why they are in there. They don't know what's happening or where their wives and families are, and they certainly don't remember their crimes. The sentencing of people for crimes committed from several decades earlier has become more apparent since the publicity of the Jimmy Saville case and since some famous BBC television and radio presenters have been under investigation and been sentenced as more of the public have come forward and reported more.

Back to the self-harm incidents, a lot of the time, they would self-harm to manipulate if they couldn't get what they wanted. We had a north African man who stitched his mouth up with big cross stitches, one each side of his mouth with thick tapestry thread cotton and the cross-thread needle. This must have been very painful, but it is surprising what people manage out of desperation. This practice is apparently quite common in the immigration detention centres when they are trying to avoid deportation.

Another tale involved two Romanians who threaded metal paper clips through their lips one each side and twisted them closed, they were also threatening to staple their eyelids shut unless they were transferred out of the prison. They did not believe they should have been put there in a sex offender establishment as they did not believe their crime was a sex related offence, despite them having been running an illegal sex slave ring with prostitution, and sex slaves and operating on a large scale which they had been for several years. They were separated and interviewed individually for an adjudication hearing and whilst out of their shared cell, the officers carried out a cell search and discovered a mobile phone in their possession. Once separated, they backed down and agreed that healthcare could remove the paper clips from their mouths. We were able to untwist them, and they actually were removed quite easily, which saved a trip out to hospital.

We had a telephone call from the wing one morning, 'Miss, we've got a prisoner who's got something stuck, he needs to come to healthcare,' I replied, 'what do you mean stuck? what has he got stuck and where is it stuck?' 'Well, it's a ring and its stuck on a part of his anatomy' The officer was obviously being polite and not wanting to say, my brain clicked in and I jokingly said, 'Oh, is it on his toe ?' then I asked , 'can he walk over ?' thinking he probably has put a ring over his penis. The officer replied, 'no. It's higher up than his toe, and I don't think he'll be able to walk over, he's in a lot of pain.' I then asked him, 'Is it his penis?' to which the relieved officer sighed and confirmed that it was, obviously grateful that I had expressed into words what the officer actually wanted to say but didn't know how. 'Send him over in a wheelchair,' I said.

The patient arrived and was highly embarrassed about what he had done. He had been sat on the examination couch with two of my nursing colleagues for the past thirty minutes with them trying various methods of removing the ring. It was a large key ring which was a double band of metal which he had put over the end of his penis three days previously. It was wedged over the end, and he had been unable to remove it. He had then been too embarrassed to report it to anybody or to ask for help. By the time we had him in healthcare his penis was very swollen and had become discoloured to a dark purple colour and was very painful.

The nurses had applied an ice pack to his penis and used lignocaine, a local anaesthetic to numb it and tried using the ring cutter we kept for removing rings from fingers from hand injuries which had become swollen. None of these methods had been successful so far. They were at the point of thinking they would have to send him in to hospital as nothing was working. He was pleading, 'oh no, please don't send me in to hospital, it's so embarrassing!' I reasoned with him, 'If you think this is embarrassing, when you get to Accident and Emergency at the hospital, they'll be even more people there to have a look.'

He was also becoming more desperate to have it removed. I asked him why he had done it. His explanation was that he was having trouble passing urine and was dribbling with urine after he had finished, and that he'd thought that it would stop the dribbling. I asked him, if it had helped, to which he replied, 'No, and now look what's happened! I didn't reply to him but thought that he had probably put it on for some sort of sexual pleasure but remained silent as he obviously did not want to tell the full story.

Strippers also use, rings to keep their erections, before they go onto the stage to perform, so he could have been using it for this purpose also, we will never know why. We did finally manage to successfully remove the ring with a pair of the podiatrist's strong metal clippers which we used as a pair of pliers. We were able to grasp the metal and unwind it with a lot of strength until it came off. 'Now, you won't be doing that again in a hurry will you?' I asked, to which he responded, 'No Miss, I'm never doing that again!' Let's hope he doesn't.

Transgender

We also had a few transgender prisoners who were allowed to dress as women despite being in a male establishment. They were allowed a choice of clothing, wigs, underwear, handbags and make up to wear. This was unfair in my mind as the male prisoners were not automatically allowed to wear their own personal clothing until they had earned the privilege by practicing good behaviour. So why should they?

They also dressed inappropriately, mainly looking like prostitutes or almost drag queens with excessive amounts of thick bright makeup and very tight short skirts and boots. One of the governors who was the Head of the Security department, rang my colleague, the Clinical Service Manager one day and asked if he could discuss the subject of 'chicken fillets' with her, he had to establish whether there would be a security risk in allowing them to have these in the prison. He had never heard of breast prosthesis being called chicken fillets before, he said, 'I've only known them to be on served on a dinner plate!'

The transgender prisoners were always requesting to be referred to the Sexual Gender Identity clinic for a sex change operation which was in Nottingham and London. None of them had been granted the operation, courtesy of the NHS yet! A requirement of having a sex change was for them to live as the opposite sex in the community for a minimum period of two years. This had always been deemed not possible whilst serving a sentence for a crime of rape to a female or to a minor.

One day I was called to a meeting to represent Healthcare. There was a panel consisting of various governors from different departments and included Security, Residential, Safer Custody, the Independent Monitoring Board, the Offender management , the parole board and the prisoner who had applied for a transfer to a female establishment to enable 'her' to live properly as a woman. The panel were video linked to a board of parole judges who wanted a decision on whether to allow this to happen.

The prisoner had a representative and put her case forward and lots of discussion ensued. I did not agree with what was happening and when asked for my input and if there were any medical reasons that would be problematic for the transfer, I had to say that medically, she was fit. I did not agree with it. Female prisoners, in the majority have been victims of rape and abuse by men. A large proportion of female prisoners have been attacked, beaten, raped, used as slaves for prostitution or become prostitutes to fund their drink and drug habits and were extremely vulnerable.

I did not believe they would allow it to happen and that they were fighting for this to be allowed. This was a male with all his genitalia intact, who now wanted to change gender. She dressed like a schoolgirl with her hair in pigtails and wore very short skirts. She had been sentenced for having raped young girls.

Anyway, she was granted the transfer and six months later, 'he/she' again committed a rape offence. This was on a female prisoner who had been abused in her past and now it had been allowed to happen again, when she should have been protected against this in a secure environment! It made my blood boil!

Why would you even consider that someone who had committed several crimes would be safe to live with vulnerable women? I am pleased to say that he did indeed get sentenced again. There have been several cases of male prisoners who are transgender and managed to be transferred into female establishments, only to then rape again. The perpetrators are dangerous people and have sexually assaulted a female inmate which is known as female perpetrated violence. They are a serious danger to incarcerated women. It happens because the words and phrase, 'gender identity' are used and common-sense identity is forgotten. The policy, 'Self Identity' means that your actual biology is forgotten and your status as a male or female is determined by your belief or claim. As I said, this is a very dangerous label to have in a place like this.

One of the prisoners who dressed as a woman, called herself, 'C C Lovecock', she dressed and acted as though she was standing on a street corner touting for business on a Saturday night out. She would always be hanging around at the end of the spur of the wing she was located on dressed in a very short tight black skirt, black fishnet stockings and boots, a black tight fitting t-shirt which she had cut the sleeves off to make smaller and show off more flesh and lower at the front to show some cleavage from her false breasts. She had grown her hair long and it was always dyed black. She always had a fully made-up face with lots of black mascara and a lot of eye makeup and she always wore very red lipstick. She had numerous piercings all over her face, eyebrows, lips and nose which she had done herself and she told us her penis was also pierced. She didn't apply to have any hormone treatments or want a referral to the gender identity clinic for any gender changing surgery, she just liked dressing as a woman or her choice of a

Woman/ prostitute. She was tall and slim and had a great pair of legs as many of the drag queens do. Her appearance depicted a gothic look, not dissimilar to an 'Amy Winehouse' lookalike. The only thing ruining it was when she opened her mouth. She had the roughest huskiest voice, deep and low and she did not sound at all feminine. She had COPD, Chronic Obstructive Pulmonary Disease caused by years of smoking. It was a shame because the rest of her carried off the look to a tee.

One of the most horrific incidents we had to deal with and was related to the transgender prisoners was this next event. One morning, on first unlock of the day, one of the officers opened the observation panel on the cell door whilst undertaking the early morning role check and discovered a prisoner on the cell floor. The door was opened quickly to reveal a man lying in a pool of his own blood, urine and faeces who was semi-conscious and almost dead. Upon closer examination it transpired he had cut off his penis and testicles! He had been fighting to be allowed to have a transgender reassignment operation and had been refused whilst serving his sentence, so he had decided to take matters into his own hands and attempt the operation himself. The officers were so shocked and traumatised by the incident upon discovering him in that state, that they had to have counselling and one of them was off work for several weeks to recover mentally from the event.

The prisoner was taken out to the local Accident and Emergency department at hospital with his penis, in a bag of ice as it was found in the cell, but the testicles were not discovered at the time of the incident so were not taken with him. They took one look at him and said they could not deal with the trauma, and he was immediately transferred to one of the London hospitals. He was seen by a locum psychiatrist in a 20-minute consultation, who was expected to undertake a full assessment of the patient and make a decision of the treatment plan. He was unable to make a fully informed decision in such a short period of time and deal with such a horrific act of self-harm, it was unfair.

Anyway, the decision was to patch him up as best they could to repair the damage. The penis was not reattached, and the scrotum was stitched up to repair it. The patient came back to healthcare after 1-2 days with a urinary catheter in situ and was actually very lucky to have survived. Some people go to extreme measures to get what they want.

I remember receiving the phone call later that morning from the wing officer who had discovered the testicles, which were hidden behind the toilet in the cell. The patient had purposely hidden them to ensure they would not be found or reattached. He asked me if we needed or wanted them in healthcare and what should they do with them? I replied, 'no, we don't need them here- what do you think we would need them for?' he really just wanted to know how to dispose of them I wasn't sure but we instructed them to dispose of them into a clinical waste bag and probably best to liaise with the police inspector who had an office based in the prison in the security department in case they were needed for any legal investigations as evidence, but I doubted it.

Apparently when the patient was transferred back to the prison following discharge from hospital, she was very proud of her new 'vagina' as she now called it and was offering to show it to the female officers who were escorting her back. They unsurprisingly, declined her offer! We nurses had to dress the wound and care for the catheter, which was eventually removed, but it was not a pretty sight, if you can imagine an empty scrotal sac stitched up in the middle, with a hole for the urine to drop out of? That prisoner was transferred out of the prison, and I don't know if she ended up having further surgery to sort out the mess, she had made of herself. She definitely was very desperate for the operation and to do such an extreme thing to herself. It is almost beyond comprehension. I heard she was advising other transgender prisoners to go ahead and try it themselves and said she didn't regret having done it to herself. As far as I know she did not receive counselling, not whilst she was in that prison anyway, but I would be surprised if she would not accept any counselling, if it was offered to her for the trauma alone would have been immense to have coped with.

Another prisoner who sticks in my mind because he was a real hoot. He made us laugh and he enjoyed shocking us and was a real performer, the more attention he received, the more outrageous he would become. He was such a character; he was a young guy, stocky and solid in build and came from an Irish travelling family. He never resorted to wearing skirts or dresses but would make alterations to his clothing. He cut the bottoms off his track suit legs to above the knee and would roll them up, very short. He would also wear the tightest pink t-shirts, or vest tops he could get hold of and bleached his hair a bright yellow- blonde colour and had it cut into a flat top style. He reminded me of a cross between 'Dafydd- the only gay in the village' character from the 'Little Britain' series and 'Kenneth'- the gay hairdresser from the 'Benidorm' TV series.

He used to come up to healthcare and discuss his make up with us, he showed us the Avon catalogue from which they were allowed to order products, and he was choosing a new foundation. He already looked orange from wearing too dark a shade for his complexion. I said to him, 'you don't want it too bright, it is supposed to look as natural as you can,' to which he proclaimed, ' But Miss, I want to look like a Dorito!' he told us if we wanted to make our eyelashes to look thicker and longer we should put talcum powder on them between coats of mascara. He always wore bright pink lipsticks and thick blusher. He was young, in his early 20's and his family of the travelling community totally disapproved of his ways of dressing and wearing makeup and had rejected and isolated him from the family which had naturally given him some issues.

He used to self-harm from time to time by making cuts to his arms with a razor, usually he would do this after he had got himself in trouble on the wing. He performed sexual favours to others for tobacco in general and illicit medication. Half an ounce of tobacco for performing oral sex and he would get himself into debt.

One day I had been called to his cell to dress his wounds and self-harming and he was very upset in tears and wouldn't let the officers near him, but he agreed to let me take a look and I patched him up and dressed the wounds. I noticed he had made a doll out of the cleaning jeye cloths which was sitting on his bed, 'did you make this I asked, picking it up, it's really clever?' I asked him, and he replied, 'Yes, It's Madeline McCann' I really didn't know what to say, but replied, 'you really shouldn't say that, it's not appropriate' but he was already angry and upset about being told off, so I didn't pursue the conversation.

Another day, he had come up to healthcare to have his piles looked at , because he had been passing some blood, so my colleagues had him lying on his side on the examination couch and just as they began the examination, of his anus, he burst into the song, 'Shine bright like a Diamond' by Rhianna! It was the funniest thing. It had them in stitches to say the least. He was such a character, and I liked him. I wonder where he ended up.

Emotional Detachment

I have been asked so many times when I tell friends or others what I do for a job, 'how do you nurse people who have done such terrible things? How do you manage to care for them? My answer is, they are still people; they are still someone's dad, brother, and son, child, nephew, uncle, and partner- despite what they have done. It is not my job to look at their crimes and to judge them. I am here to do my job and that is to care for them. It is definitely best not to pry into the crimes they have committed, or to question why they committed them. We nurse them for who they are as a person, at the time and as best we can, day in and day out and repeatedly sometimes for the same conditions or complaints with the saying in the root of our minds, 'theirs not to reason why, but to do or die' from The Charge of the Light Brigade poem by Lord Tennyson. In other words, it did not matter what they had done it was their reason, and our duty, not to question why, but to treat what we were presented with at the time.

I had been taught with the view that, none of us were angels, but we certainly did our best. In hindsight and with the experience I now have of over 30 years of nursing, I know I am allowed to feel uncomfortable, and afraid, I make mistakes, and I learn from them, and I am humbled every step of the way. I strive to be a better nurse and person. Sometimes, I feel anxious and inadequate and concerned I don't have enough knowledge or the right answers. But I also know I should not take too much stock of what others think of me, since everyone has their faults and imperfections.

I learnt during my training that, 'the function of a good nurse is to care for the sick. A good nurse will treat her patients with kindness and understanding, without ever getting too involved with their suffering. This detachment is often called hardness by those outside the profession. It is not hardness; it is our defence against being torn to emotional shreds by the work we are called upon to do. I read a book once, 'The nurse who bleeds for her patients will find herself bleeding in vain, she will get more reward from caring for them.'

We had another prisoner who was a prolific self-harmer and inserted parts of a radio into his open wounds in his arms He pushed the retractable aerial into his arm from his elbow where he had made the wound all the way to his wrist, he also inserted a parker pen and a straightened out paperclip. He regularly swallowed batteries and blades and also took small alarm clock apart and swallowed parts of it in order to get sent out to hospital, to have some of them that were possible to extract, removed.

He arrived up in healthcare the morning after the Eurovision song contest, he had seen on TV the previous evening, for his morning see to take medication. He arrived having drawn on his face with a black marker pen, a beard, a moustache and thick black eyebrows and then used a pink highlighter pen to create lipstick on his mouth but not very neatly resulting in looking like a clown. He announced very loudly for all the others in the waiting room and meds queue to hear, 'I'm the Eurovision Queen!'

Sexual Acts

We had a small prisoner from the Philippines' who was a known arsonist and part of his sentence was for setting a fire in a hotel, but he was also a sex offender, He was a vulnerable prisoner who used to regularly perform sexual favours to the older prisoners until he got caught one day in the gardens, amongst the rose bushes by one of the officers. He was giving oral sex to an older prisoner who was paying him for it and was in his late eighties.

The elderly prisoner would buy him new clothes, as payment for his services from one of the catalogues they were allowed to buy from, called, 'get the label.com, 'he was always very proud to show you his new clothes of labelled brands. At least he was smartly dressed in trendy clothes of the latest fashion.

If they were going to have sex, they would usually be caught in the act in the bathrooms or the showers on the wings, or more normally in their cells. The officers whilst performing their observation checks open the observation panels in the doors and have witnessed many a sight. One man had attached his chair to the bed and was backing himself onto one of the chair legs; others have 'accidentally slipped and fallen' onto the handle of a toilet brush which has ended up in their rectum! I don't honestly know how they think that their story can be believed when all of a sudden, their underwear falls off, and they slip at the exact precise angle for it to end up, up there!

One of the more recent reports which came from an intelligence report submitted by one of the officers through the security department was that during the night checks the prisoner was observed squatting in the middle of his cell completely naked bouncing up and down on what looked like a deodorant can/bottle inserted up his bum. This was the second incident with the said prisoner that had happened within a week. It was suggested that this was intentional as he knew when the checks were being conducted and knew that there was a female officer present. It was unlikely to have been coincidental.

One of my colleagues who worked in pharmacy, had just started in her job and was working her first shift on her own. The young prisoner came up to the hatch and passed her a note, which said, ' HELP, I've got an aerosol can stuck up my arse' she was so astounded she told him to go and take a seat while she called the other side of healthcare and arranged for the nurses to go over to see him. He headed over to the chairs in the waiting area and cautiously lowered himself onto the seat, not surprisingly!

The most bizarre object I had come across being inserted into a rectum was an orange, not a small tangerine, a full-sized orange, why? I don't have the answer, but as we couldn't remove it in healthcare, we had to send him out to hospital.

We also had a frequent visitor attending healthcare with bladder issues and urinary tract infections, (UTI). He had inserted a paper clip which he had first straightened out, into his urethra in his penis and I don't know how he had managed it, but he hadn't told us what he had done. He had presented in healthcare with symptoms of a UTI. He had blood in his urine, pain when passing urine, frequency and difficulty with emptying his bladder. After several course of antibiotics which appeared to be clearing up his symptoms it would return again soon after. As he was a young man, we sent him out to hospital for a scan to see if something else was going on, and the paper clip was revealed on the scan to have moved up his urethra and was then lodged in his bladder.

The hospital was prepared to try and remove it via a uroscopy, but he refused and so it was left there. It was likely to have eventually disintegrated with the urine which should erode it away, but he was also at risk of it perforating his bladder. He would not be persuaded to have the procedure, so he returned to the prison, and had no further issues with us. He was transferred to another prison, so I never found out about future problems.

I think we were subjected to more than a normal amount of people presenting in healthcare with symptoms concerning their penises. This was most likely due to the nature of them being sex offenders as some did seem to be rather obsessed with their genitalia. Since having left the prison, I have had the odd problem which men have presented with at the doctors surgery, where I now work, concerning their genitals, but these are normal conditions which occur in the general population.

I had one man present in clinic and request that I measure his penis in its full state of arousal and fully erect as he wanted the documentation made in his medical notes for him to provide to the courts. He was appealing his sentence and attempting to prove that there was no way he could have raped the person that had accused him of the act with the size of his penis.

Another came into my clinic saying he had a problem with excessive masturbation. That he was masturbating between 6-8 times a day and that he couldn't stop. I had not come across these sorts of issues previously in my career and it could have been that he was trying to incite a reaction from me by telling me this, or he could have been telling the truth. I don't think this is a normal conversation that the general public have with health professionals on an everyday basis, but it certainly initiated our conversations over lunch with my colleagues.

I advised him that maybe he should start to reduce the times he did it and wean himself down like with any addiction. I also asked him why he was worried about it and thought if he wasn't harming anyone else or himself, why did it matter as long as he was doing it in his own privacy. He told me he was concerned that he may run out of sperm if he kept masturbating excessively and that he probably wanted to have more children when he got out. I then was able to reassure him that this wouldn't happen, so at least I had answered his question and addressed his real concerns and literally then left him to it!

We used to have a GUM clinic which was set up and run by a visiting consultant in the healthcare centre. GUM stands for Genito-Urinary Medicine. The consultant was female, and she had to be chaperoned by one of us nurses due to the nature of the situation. I was the chaperone on this occasion, and we had a very concerned man in his late twenties for a consultation. He was worried that his penis was bent when it was erect and looked not dissimilar to a banana. He was disturbed by it and wanted to have surgery to correct it. He was not in pain with it, and it was fully functional, he just did not like the shape of it. It hadn't just happened either he had had this for quite some time, and he did not confess to having had forceful intercourse.

The consultant began to explain about how the reservoirs of blood can become fractured and leak into other areas within the penis and that this was likely the cause of the bent shape. Whilst she was explaining this, he had stood up, dropped his trousers and underwear and began playing with his penis in order to get it erect to show the doctor what he meant. She had not yet got to the examination part of the consultation., and we both were very surprised that he was actually doing this whilst he was still being spoken to.

She then asked him to stop doing this so that she could examine him properly on the examination couch and advised that it did not have to be erect and that it would be harder to examine when fully erect. She would be able to feel for any potential fracture of the penis better, when it is in a flaccid state. He just seemed to ignore her and continued his actions and kept saying he wanted to show us what he meant.

I had to step in and take control of the situation as he was just not listening. I clearly said to him, if he didn't stop right then and there and listen to the consultant then the consultation was over, and I would call one of the officers in to ask him to leave. He then complied with what we had asked him to do. He was referred to the hospital for potential surgery to correct it, but it would have been very unlikely that they would accept him for corrective surgery in view of the fact that it would have been for an aesthetic purpose and not due to any dysfunctional ability.

They have also been openly masturbating in front of the doors when they know the checks are being conducted and knowing there are female officers on duty performing the checks. Whether they perform to intimidate or to stimulate their excitement of being caught in the act, whatever the reason, it is not pleasant for the younger female or male officers to have to witness this. Some of them do this in the segregation unit because they know they are more regularly checked, but thankfully the officers usually open the door flap first to check and can prevent us from having to witness this.

I will never forget the time one of my colleagues was asked if she would like to 'have a little suck of it?' This was one of the young offenders, honestly, the audacity of them! My colleague was a very experienced nurse and was in her late fifties at the time, she was doing the initial assessments of the new prisoners in reception, and it was whilst we had the young offenders in the prison. She was going through the initial questions asking about previous medical history, conditions and medications etc, when she noticed the prisoner had his hands inside the front of his jogging bottoms and was holding his penis. She had asked him a question, when he flopped his penis out and looked her in the eye, then he asked if she would like to, 'give it a little kiss' and, 'would she like a little suck on it? 'At first, she was so shocked she didn't believe what he had said, but once she registered it, she jumped up and pointing towards the door she shouted at him to 'get out'.

The officer heard and jumped up asking her what was wrong, and she then had to repeat what he had asked her. The prisoner was taken down to the segregation unit and was actually charged for this, but she did have to report him, and he underwent an adjudication. She also had to attend a court case in order for this to happen and he was transferred out of the prison, which is probably what he wanted in the first place as he didn't want to be in that particular prison.

More recently I was told a story by one of the younger officers whose colleague had checked through the hatch and found three prisoners, having anal sex, all joined together, which was a shocking experience and not something you could easily forget having witnessed that!

Animals

Acts I cannot understand or accept are those of bestiality, this is sexual acts with and cruelty to animals. So, we had a patient who used dogs for his sexual gratification. He would re-home them from rescue centres and his preference was for the larger breeds, Retrievers, Labradors and German shepherds, he apparently used peanut butter applied to his anus to encourage the dogs, which then stimulated him, and I will leave the rest to your imagination! Diabolical I know it damages your mind thinking about it. I will never understand how their minds work! He was actually released for a time and then recalled completing another sentence, when he appeared at the medication hatch, I couldn't believe he was back again. I said, 'oh no, what have you done to have landed up back in here?' then, before he could respond, I quickly followed on with, 'actually, please don't answer that, I don't want to know'.

The prison in conjunction with a greyhound rescue centre set up a fostering programme for the prisoners to care for, socialise and retrain the retired greyhounds from racing, whilst awaiting their new homes and adoption. The facilities which were built, were amazing, with beautiful kennels, and heated, raised, off the floor beds. The dogs would be exercised around the prison grounds in their colourful coats. Animals need the handlers to accept responsibility and teach them social interaction and care for them, some of whom did not have caring backgrounds and had malfunctioning families and disjointed upbringing. It was a fantastic idea and provided the therapeutic benefits animals can give to humans. Unfortunately, after 2-3 years it was closed down. I never knew if it was a rumour or the truth that a prisoner had been having sex with the dogs. I hope a rumour, but the programme was ended, and quite rightly so.

We also had one who had a duck which was found in his cell, which he had attempted to boil in his kettle. I assume with the intention of eating it. I don't even want to think about if he had done anything else to it first. I bumped into him outside healthcare one weekend, mid-morning hovering in the corridor. He was under the radar of Security and was suspected of trading his medication, so I questioned him, 'what are you doing here?' he answered, 'I just came to collect my meds, Miss', I told him, 'well you are the wrong side of the prison for your meds, aren't you? But now you're here, what were you doing with that duck in your cell?' he answered, 'what duck Miss? How do you know about that? I was just keeping it as a pet' so I asked him, 'well, why did you put it in your kettle then?' he turned on his heel, made a quick exit and practically ran off then as he didn't know what else to say to me.

Most of the prisoners were very kind to the abundance of ducks we had in the grounds. They were constantly hatching ducklings and would start with up to 15 cute fluffy babies which would dwindle in numbers rapidly usually due to the rats getting them at night. Sometimes they would fall down the drains and you would see the prisoners trying to rescue them from the drains. The prisoners would throw bread out of the cell windows for the ducks, birds and pigeons, but this encouraged the rats that were fed immensely well and became very big.

One year the numbers of rats became out of control. They became very brave and unafraid of humans; you could see them grazing in the grounds like guinea pigs (without the tails) in broad daylight. They made no attempt to run off or hide when anyone walked past. I always wonder if it was anything to do with them getting a little bit of Methadone in the drains, when we washed the last drops of a container down the sink? An officer told me he had once witnessed a pigeon which had flown into the barbed wire at the top of the fencing and died. It had been stripped and eaten within minutes by the rats which climbed up the chain mesh fencing to get to it. I had heard, for every rat above the ground you saw, there would be another ten below ground in their nests. It was very unnerving when you went through the grounds at night. Eventually though the prison employed a new pest control service, and more traps and poison was put down and they have diminished.

I had a pair of wood pigeons who nested twice a year outside my office window. They had built the nest in the wire netting fence which was covered in a vine and fairly camouflaged in the summer. They always laid 2 eggs and raised the squabs very well each time. We had an elderly patient who was brought over to healthcare every evening for his insulin injection and was pushed in the wheelchair by another prisoner. He was suffering with dementia and could not self-care or remember to give his insulin to himself, but he took great pleasure in seeing those pigeons growing every day in their nest, He had once kept racing pigeons when he was younger and always told me about them, facts and stories that he remembered well. I would help him to pull himself up from the wheelchair; by holding onto the bars of the heavy gate so he could see them in the nest.

Another elderly man also suffering with dementia had served in the navy in his younger years and thought he was on a ship; he thought he could hear the waves crashing up to his window and that his cell was a cabin. He had laid out pictures he had taken from magazines of three women one of them being the actress Joanna Lumley, on his bed and then he had put crisps and biscuits on their mouths and told me he was feeding his girls.

In the last year of my working there we had more access to help and resources through the NHS trust, for the dementia patients and one man was issued with a dementia cat which was a furry toy cat, very lifelike and it meowed and purred. For the most part, he loved it and held it as a comfort. He had also been found to have thrown it across his cell, just as well it wasn't real!

Medications- Administration and Compliance

As a prison nurse a large part of your role involves administering medications also known as 'giving out the meds', in some other establishments it is a major role and can quite commonly, take the whole morning. If there is Methadone involved, there can be up to 100 patients who are in receipt of prescribed Methadone. This is an Opiate Substitute treatment and helps to keep the patients who have substance misuse history to be stable, stops them suffering from withdrawal effects and helps prevent them from continuing to misuse and take illicit drugs or medications.

The nurses could then have a couple of hours free after lunch for clinics and then they would restart the evening medication round. This is due to the risk status of having 'in possession' medication. In the higher category prisons, called, the local prisons, (where they intake people straight from court hearings when they have been sentenced, or from police custody, whilst awaiting sentencing and have not been granted bail) which are classed as Category B prisons and Cat A prisons, they are very unlikely to be given many, if any, of their own medications in possession, due to the risks being much higher. The risk being attempting to overdose due to the imminent stress and trauma of receiving the sentence and this is heightened when it is their first sentence.

The other risk is that of trading their medications with others either freely or the more vulnerable may be the subject of bullying and be forced to obtain them for the benefit of others to trade.

In this prison, the pharmacy teamwork, extremely hard and we tried to have as many patients as possible taking responsibility for their own medications. All new arrivals had an 'In possession medication risk assessment' undertaken when they arrived in reception. They were assessed by the nurses. They could be reviewed and changed as and when necessary. This could be for various reasons including a notice from Security indicating that they have received intelligence about the prisoner trading his medications.

We, in healthcare would then carry out a medication compliance check and if they did not have the correct amount of tablets or appeared to be trading them, such as having taken them out of the original packaging, or having removed the labels with their names on, or stored them into smaller packaging, or the tablets had been wrapped in cling film or put into small pots, then they would be reviewed. The medication would be either reduced, then stopped, stopped immediately or they would be put onto 'see to take', also known as supervised consumption of medication as their administration of medication method.

Compliance of Medication

The patient may be unable to take responsibility for taking their own medications especially if they have recently been sentenced for the first time and they are badly affected by the shame and humiliation about their crime that their families or loved ones will have to endure. We had mainly a vulnerable person population in the prison that had poor or no coping strategies in life and had been transferred to the establishment because they had been bullied in other mainstream jails, they were at risk of overdose when things didn't go their way and were also at risk of being bullied for their medications.

There were also some prisoners of the older generation, some with dementia/ Alzheimer's that could not cope or just simply could not remember to take their medications. Then there were those with a history of trading their medications or attempting to divert their medications to enable trading of them.

There were others, who were at risk of overdose or those at risk of suicide and had an ACCT document opened on them. This could be opened by any member of staff working in the prison, regardless of if they were employed by the prison service or not, if they had a concern that a prisoner may be at risk of self-harm. The Assessment, Care in Custody Teamwork (ACCT) is the care planning process for those prisoners identified as being at risk of self-harm or suicide and ensures that a process is in place and certain actions are followed to reduce the risk. Being on an ACCT could mean that their medications would be removed from their possession and administered as a 'see to take' medication. The ACCT document does not always result in the removal of meds; the risk has to be assessed. If they have no intention of taking an overdose and no previous history of overdose, and no intention of taking their life, the risk is low. It may be that they self-harm by cutting themselves, or another method.

Another reason for checking their compliance can be that they are refusing to take their medications for various reasons. This can be displayed in their behaviour when they become angry or upset at the rules of the prison or of the judicial system. The reasons could be of not being granted parole at their latest parole hearing, having just been adjudicated or 'nicked' for negative behaviour or that they had lost some of their privileges or rights, and therefore their status, or their 'canteen items', their TV or their jobs within the prison. They would often use manipulative behaviour and become threatening with it. Some would retreat into themselves, and some would refuse to take their medication. They saw it as a rebellious act but did not seem to understand it was themselves, they were harming, not us. But if the cause had stemmed from them initially (as a result of negative behaviour) then it was a way of self-punishment.

Another self-harm method included refusal to eat, I will come back to this later. We also had a lot of patients with long term conditions who took medications to reduce and maintain their Blood Pressure within normal parameters, for Diabetes and for Cardiac and Respiratory conditions. These patients always caused us concern when they refused to comply and take their medications over long periods.

Administration of Medications

All of the controlled drugs were categorised as 'not in possession' and had to be administered by two healthcare professionals and the records kept in the controlled drugs register. The prisoners were regularly caught attempting to divert their medication because it was highly valuable as a source of tradable income. The nurse had to be constantly vigilant whilst administering the 'see to take' medication and the prisoner had to open his mouth to show that it had been swallowed. This was easier said than done as some were very quick and clever, pushing it up between the back teeth and cheeks, often hiding it under the tongue and occasionally keeping it in their hands.

They used all sorts of charm and pleasantries to the nurses and pharmacy staff and were very chatty to try and divert the nurse's attention away from being vigilant and watching them intently. I remember one lad telling me all about pouching his methadone in his cheek, I said. 'Wow, how on earth can someone do that, it would be impossible surely?' he answered, 'I'll show you, Miss', so he tipped his 40mls methadone into his mouth , appeared to have swallowed it, opened his mouth wide to show me it was empty, then swallowed the 150mls water , I had given him, showed me his mouth again, grinned at me and then re-opened his mouth to show me the original 40mls of green methadone undiluted, still in his mouth, Incredible. 'That's amazing, ' I said, very clever, ' but, we are not penguins, and we don't regurgitate our food , so, now you're nicked and you will be starting on a reduction of your methadone because you are clearly not taking it yourself and selling it '. So, although they are clever, they can also be stupid.

Another incident which I clearly remember was involving the buprenorphine tablets, also known as subutex. They were an alternative opiate substitute treatment to methadone and had to be crushed and dissolved under the tongue. We did not maintain patients, long term on this because of the high attempts to divert it. It has a high value for trading.

When we administered this the prisoner had to drink water first to ensure his mouth was clear, because they had been known to put plastic at the back of the throat to catch the powder on. Then we would watch them tip it under the tongue at the front of the mouth. They had to sit on a chair with their hands on show at all times on their legs or sit on their hands and were on camera surveillance. We would then check halfway through that it was still under the tongue, because they could also push bits into tooth cavities or up into the cheek and hold it there between the gum and cheek. We had to see if we could see their tongue moving around, while it was dissolving sub lingually, and they were not allowed to talk. Then we would check it had dissolved and there was no remaining residue, then they would take more water.

We had high suspicions of diverting and previous recorded history of this in his medical records. He actually had managed to wipe some onto his hand from his mouth and smeared it onto his ID identity card which he was wearing around his neck. When he left the room, I asked the attending officers to stop him and remove his ID card, he went mad, protesting loudly and knew he had been caught. I then removed the smeared tablet, dissolved it into water and tested it with the drug screening kits, lo and behold it was a positive result to the presence of Buprenorphine. He was adjudicated and reduced off his prescription. I was happy, to have stopped another one with illicit trading of medication.

Prescribed medication is used as currency and can get people into all sorts of trouble when it is misused. There are a lot of bullies inside the prison who will put all sorts of pressure onto others to get a supply which they will use to trade.

The main concern from a healthcare professional with a registration is to protect that hard earned qualification, which we have all worked damn hard to obtain and want to retain it. I am also a Nurse Prescriber, so it is of the highest concern to me to ensure that the correct patient gets the correct medication at the correct time. This sounds simple enough, but it is an ongoing, ever-changing task to keep up with.

I have discussed the in-possession status of medication and how that can change in an instant when a circumstance changes. We have to assess patients and their responsibilities of taking their medications correctly, but when they become desperate or are put under pressure they will often succumb to the bullying and give their medication away or will use it to trade. This is not actual cash, but money can be transferred or paid into either theirs or others outside bank accounts or used for their canteen items, which is their weekly purchased order of extras they have access to buy, in addition to the food they receive from the servery for example toiletries and any authorised extras such as coffee or vapes, which used to be tobacco before the prisons went nonsmoking.

Spice

Healthcare used to provide Nicotine Replacement Therapy patches and lozenges and tablets on occasion, and they would be used to trade. Sometimes they will want the use of a mobile phone which are often smuggled in and used to trade with outside contacts to obtain drugs and more so nowadays, Novel Psychoactive Substances (NPS) such as 'spice'. Spice is a broad name for these new, synthetically manufactured substances which are causing a huge problem in most prisons across the country. These substances are also named mamba, man down, zombie, bird killer, rice, Katie price, pot Poruri to name a few.

For the healthcare professional, the most concerning thing is that there is no protocol on how to treat it specifically because there are so many ever-changing forms of it. The symptoms of presentation of its effects differ greatly and you can only treat what you have presenting in front of you at the time. There is no specific antidote to counteract it. Some people will have a tachycardia, a very fast heart rate and others will be bradycardic, which is the opposite with a very slow heart rate. They can have either slow or fast respiratory rates of their breathing and either a high or a low blood pressure.

It does generally make them display very bizarre behaviour, an example of which was two men in another establishment, stuffed newspaper down the front of their t-shirts and set fire to themselves in their cells, one of them died as a result. It took a long time to get the door open to release them. The second one suffered excruciating extensive burns. It is very scary stuff and the worst of it is that we and the prison officers are exposed to it as we are expected to enter the cells to monitor and treat them. Just by standing at the doorway, if they have been vaping it, the smoke vape in the atmosphere makes you feel very dizzy and lightheaded and quite weird very quickly and even when you have had minimal exposure. It has made officers unwell and even one of the dogs passed out and had to refrained from returning to duty for six days.

When the prison was informed that we were going to be a nonsmoking prison, a lot of the prisoners started to stock buy tobacco and ordering was rationed, more so that normally, but there were lots of non- smoking prisoners who also started to order tobacco so that they could hide it as the value would be increasing rapidly as it was to become to be in short supply and sought after. Some were bullied into buying it to hold for the smokers and traders in their cells so the dealers would not get caught with a stock of it. Once the date arrived and we became smoke free, the prisoners resorted to smoking other things, these included tea bags, banana skins, the NRT patches rolled up and plant leaves from the gardens.

They were already known to smoke the buprenorphine analgesic patches when they were desperate and addicted to opiates.

A few months after the date, there were a few large stashes of tobacco found; one had been buried in the grounds in the gardens amongst the flower beds and another large stash in the recycling bins. We had to watch out for 'throw over's' as well, these would arrive over the fencing and be drugs which had been concealed in dead pigeons, ducks, rats and tennis balls. , In the inner city jails people have even attached drugs to money coins which are small enough to fit through the fencing links.

Prisoners are extremely resourceful and have a lot of time on their hands to think and plot. When they want to use illicit medications, they are very clever and should not be underestimated. They scrape the buprenorphine patches and flake it into their tobacco to smoke or would soak it in boiling water to dissolve the opiate from the patch and drink it or some have been known to try and inject it. With the co-codamol and dihydrocodeine tablets, they would crush them and dissolve or mix with water and filtered using either bread or a jeye cloth to separate the contents to produce the opiate-based liquid.

They are ingenious and would brew alcohol known as 'hooch' using bread or marmite as the yeast base and lots of fruit, mainly oranges and once they had found a suitable container which could easily be sourced, such as a bottle of squash which would suffice and was readily available from the canteen orders, they were able to brew the hooch. It actually looked like vomit in a bottle because it was a dark brownish, orangey colour with lumps of bread and fruit floating in it. It had to be opened very carefully because it would explode if it was still fermenting. I have heard that they have been known to have been found brewing it in the radiators of their cells! I said they were clever. We had a sniffer dog that has been trained to detect it. The random searches were conducted alongside the suspicious ones, more frequently around Christmas time. Usually, it was a successful search and always resulted in some finds. These people if and when caught would end up with a little holiday, down the block (seg).

It was pretty potent stuff, and we had several cases of alcohol intoxication. We also had to be very careful with the hand gel we ordered in healthcare as some has an alcohol content and could be stolen and drunk. During Covid and the ordering in of the Personal Protective Equipment (PPE), we were so busy and used PPE constantly. We had to ensure strict hand hygiene measures were in place with the supply of hand gel placed in the waiting room, on the desks, in each consultation room, at the entrance and exit of each of the healthcare departments that we had not noticed the high 80% alcohol it contained. This could have caused some issues if it had been consumed. I only noticed it and looked at the label on the bottle because the gloves we were using when we were giving the Covid vaccinations disintegrated after using the alcohol-gel to clean them.

Self-harm – ACCT – Safer Custody

If a prisoner has voiced intent to harm themselves or appear to have become very low in mood, or depressed, enough to raise concern. It then places the patient under more supervision than normal and interviews are held on a regular basis by the wing officers, a senior officer or a custodial manager and can include a member of the mental health team, healthcare nurses, chaplaincy, the prisoners key worker or anyone involved in that person's care and wellbeing.

The Safer Custody team are prison staff members who are trained to spot those prisoners who are at risk of bullying, suicide and self-harm. The team has a responsibility to identify and support those prisoners who are at risk of harm to themselves, to others and from others. The frequency of these checks on that person is determined at these meetings and they can be placed onto a 'constant watch' which involves an officer who is stationed outside the cell door which is left open at all times and a gate is used across the entrance. This gate may be shielded with a plastic screen to protect the officer, depending on the prisoner's behaviour as sometimes they can spit or throw urine or faeces or any loose objects from the cell at the officer.

Constant watch means an officer literally sits there for 24 hours a day. They obviously change stints with another throughout the period as it can be very taxing, and distressing to be subjected to abuse, verbal and physical as well as mentally when they observe someone cutting themselves, swallowing items, defecating, or even masturbating in front of them. They have to keep watch of that person to ensure they are safe. If they attempt a suicide for example the making of a ligature to attempt to hang themselves, or swallowing medications they have managed to obtain, the officer will alert others, and they will have to enter the cell to stop them succeeding in their self-harm attempt. Not all of the wings have these 'Safe cells' so prisoners had quite often to be moved to another location, either on another wing, or to the segregation unit.

Some of these men become very angry and will destroy their cells. I witnessed a majorly damaged cell in the segregation unit where the prisoner had blocked the toilet and flooded the cell and managed to cut out a breeze block from the wall. He had ripped up the wooden cupboard and smashed it into smaller pieces. He had then spent all night posting it through the flap on the door which he had also broken the glass out of, until the whole cupboard was outside of his cell in the corridor.

Segregation Unit

All prisons will have a segregation unit, known as 'the seg' or 'the block'. This is where prisoners are confined in isolation or segregated in individual cells, usually due to misbehaviour, failure to comply to the rules or orders, violence to others which can be other prisoners or towards the officers or other staff working in the prison, bullying behaviour, and sometimes due to the risk they pose to themselves. If they are under threat from others, for being in debt and owing for whatever they have borrowed or illicitly obtained or traded. this is usually illicit drugs or medications, but it can be a PlayStation or a vape or an item they haven't returned to the owner or paid for. Sometimes it could be because they have provided information against another person and 'grassed them up'.

If they are violent, they have to be restrained and removed from their cells under guided force. They are taken to the segregation unit also known as 'the Seg' or 'the block'. The Seg is the confined segregation unit, CSU, and they are kept in isolation for a period until they calm down and agree to be compliant and return to the wing. If they won't, they may end up eventually getting transferred to another prison. The use of force process is known as C and R, (Control and Restraint) and consists of a team of officers who are dressed, in riot gear, known as getting 'kitted up' for the restraint.

The riot gear consisted of black overalls and included helmets, boots, gloves, a body shield, batons and handcuffs. The staff must first attempt to de-escalate the situation, and they must release holds and restraints as soon as it is deemed safe to do so. The healthcare team, nurses were called to these situations within daily working hours to be part of the assessment of a prisoner who was under restraint as some of the holds can potentially cause injury. The most dangerous is when someone is being restrained in a prone restraint position, which is lying flat, face down, and with an officer on his back, as there is a risk of suffocation.

We had to assess that the airway was clear. In most cases, 9/10, the prisoner would be shouting and screaming abuse at the officers and was definitely, clearly breathing with an unobstructed airway. We would go when it was a planned restraint, usually if someone had barricaded themselves into a cell, but other times, if for instance a fight broke out on the wings, there wouldn't be time for a planned, restraint, so there would be no team, and no nurses to observe.

Some men were very strong and would sometimes require a six man unlock. The most memorable six man unlock, I saw, was in a Category A prison on a young man; he was in his early twenties and was in for the murder of his girlfriend and her new boyfriend. He had followed them home, broken in with a forced entry and stabbed them both to death. I had to interview him regarding his substance misuse methadone prescription and treatment. I watched from the cell door. He was instructed to retreat to the back of the cell and to kneel down with his back to the officers and the door and put his head in front of his knees on the floor. He then had to place his hands behind his back. When he was in that position and remained motionless, the officers entered and put the handcuffs on him and assisted him to stand, he was then walked to the stairs and guided down, standing and negotiated the stairs sideways.

Some prisoners may attempt to throw themselves forwards down the stairs with the prisoner officers attached. He was a six man unlock. He was put into the interview room, into the back section which was another small room with a solid metal door which had a clear screen, for him to sit behind, with several small holes in the screen to allow me to hear him and talk to him through. When they entered the back room, the procedure was then carried out in reverse, and the handcuffs removed. I wanted him to sign the treatment plan we had agreed on regarding the methadone, but I had to remove the middle of the biro pen, the tube containing the ink and the pen nib, so it was narrow enough to push it through one of the holes in the plastic screen for him to use, to sign the plan. He did comply fully with this, but I remember thinking, Crikey! This is like a scene from Hannibal Lector!

Another act the prisoners would undertake especially if they were protesting about being kept in the segregation unit, down the block, was a 'dirty protest 'where they would defecate and smear it over the cell walls, sometimes writing unsavoury language with the faeces across the walls. The officers would sometimes get it thrown at them when they opened the cell doors. Sometimes they would get urine or semen thrown at them or be spat at when opening the door. That is why they are always taught to check first, before opening the cell door, by looking through the hatch and to check the prisoner is visible in case he could jump on you in an attack. Sometimes this behaviour could be caused by being unwell mentally and them having a psychotic episode.

Some are taken to the block because they have been involved in fights on the wing. A lot of the time, they get themselves put down the block from choice. If they have gotten themselves into debt on the wing and are in trouble, and owe money, they will purposely misbehave. They may be rude, aggressive or threatening to the officers. They may simply refuse to be 'locked up' or 'banged up' i.e. return to their cells when it was time to and put up a fight.

Sometimes they would do the opposite. They may barricade themselves in their cells and refuse to come out. They would cover the observation panel, through which the officers check them and make it impossible for them to be seen. They would block the door with any pieces of furniture, cupboards and chairs in the cell that was moveable to stop entry into the cell. All the beds were fixed and on the original older side of the prison, the metal beds were all bolted to the floor.

When they resort to this behaviour, the prison will send an officer trained in negotiation down to the cell, who will spend hours trying to talk the prisoner into surrendering and coming out of his free will. If this fails, then the team will get kitted up into the C & R kit as previously mentioned to perform a restrained move. These have now more recently been renamed as use of force moves and the restraints are called guided holds. If the prisoner doesn't come willingly, they will be removed from the cell and taken to the seg.

In theory this sounds very easy, but it requires planning, precision, good organisation and teamwork. In recent years, the use of all staff wearing body worn cameras has come into force. The team wear the cameras and the whole event is recorded. This is invaluable for evidence when the prisoner later attempts to sue the prison for alleged injuries they claim to have sustained. This is where the nurses role in healthcare comes in. If there is to be a 'planned move' which is the removal of a prisoner from his cell, under restraint. If use of force, is applied because the prisoner is non-compliant and resisting to come willingly, then the nurse has to observe to ensure that the prisoner is not at risk of suffocation when the officers have to pin them down in a hold.

I found this to be very exciting and the adrenaline was up, because the officers were 'kitted up' in the full riot gear. Their safety was paramount and the prisoner to have got to this stage enough to require the use of force sometimes was found to have an incredible strength from within with his adrenaline pumping and would fight the officers off using pre-made weapons. These they had fashioned from pieces of furniture from in their cells. I witnessed a guy wrap a metal chair leg around an officer's legs and bend it as he tried to trap the officer.

If they refused to open the door of the cell and come out and surrender, the officers would burst the cell open and rush in pinning the prisoner with their shields to the back wall until all the officers were able to get hold of him and restrain him. They would then be able to get the handcuffs on and get him under control.

I saw how they actually took the heavy metal door off its' hinges with a jack and removed it fully to enable them to get into the cell to restrain the prisoner. It always makes me think of the film, 'The Italian Job,' when Michael Cain says, 'You're only supposed to blow the bloody doors off '

Mental Health

I witnessed this when we had a patient who was very unwell with mental health and had to be sectioned under the mental health act. He had to be restrained in order to get him onto the prison transport vehicle, known as, 'the bus' in order to take him to a psychiatric secure facility for treatment. The manoeuvre was very well performed, and I watched the footage later. The officers spoke to him all of the time to let him know what was happening. I cannot see how else they would have been able to get him out and onto the bus because we are no longer allowed to sedate patients with injections without their consent which is essentially classed as against their will. He was so paranoid by the time he had been sectioned; he refused to take any medication off anyone. The sectioning process can take time to arrange due to the difficulty of getting the psychiatrists into the prison and the availability of them. He also had not eaten properly for several weeks because he was convinced everyone was attempting to poison him and that the food was contaminated.

We had another patient suffering with paranoia. He kept asking for tin foil to cover his head to stop the aliens he believed were reading his thoughts and he wanted to block them by using the aluminium tin foil. he would not take his hat off because he thought they would be able to take over his mind. He had managed to get a metal colander from the wing kitchen and was wearing this on his head.

We also had a man in his late sixties who was serving an IPP sentence, this is an indeterminate public protection sentence, which basically has no release date and can be longer than a life sentence if the parole board feel you would not be safe to be let put into society and that the public would be at risk. A pretty depressing thought that he may never get released.

These men did not have an awful, lot to look forward to and actually did well to keep going.

It was a shame because he was a fantastic artist and had painted many brightly coloured pictures which were beautiful and he had given them to the mental health department because he had received a lot of attention, help and therapy from them. He had raped a woman and then murdered her then, if that wasn't bad enough, he had continued to have sex with her dead body several days later. He had kept her rolled up in a carpet when her body was found.

He became psychotic over some time, I think it related to him having recently been in front of the parole board for his, latest hearing yet again and he had been refused a transfer to a Cat D open prison, where he would have had less restrictions imposed. He would have been allowed to go out to work during the day, outside of the prison and return at night which would have given him more freedom.

Parole

The parole hearings were held to see if a prisoner was deemed fit to be released or to be trusted more, to allow them to live in less confined conditions. They were held approximately every two years in front of a panel. They had to submit their case to the board, and it was very stressful for them. For him to be refused again was a big blow when that was the only thing, he had been clinging to in the hope that he could move forward and progress to keep him going. It could be between eighteen months to three years between the hearings.

He had stopped taking his antipsychotic medications and had begun to have paranoid thoughts. The mental health team were called one day to try and help him and persuade him to get out from under his bed where he was hiding. He was a very big bloke, in his late sixties and had fairly poor mobility. He was naked and had drawn all over his face with a black permanent marker pen. He was taken to the seg and sectioned under the mental health act. When he was transferred, he did agree to take an oral sedative medication to keep him calm for the journey and he was escorted with one of the mental health nurses and the officers. He was transported in a prison van; they took some of the seats out of and put a mattress on the floor which he laid on and slept. This made the nurse feel very nervous because she had experienced this procedure once before with a sedated patient in a restraint vest, which was similar to a strait jacket and in prone position, face down. They are a greater risk of suffocation in this position and this man who was being transferred had several underlying conditions already. The good news is that he made it unscathed and safely to his destination and the mental health nurse returned very relieved.

Creativity

The prisoners were very creative and there were some remarkable paintings, drawings and murals around the prison on the walls and in the corridors which brightened up the place. They also made a lot of craft with matchsticks in their cell, some incredible, photo frames, jewellery boxes, clock surrounds and models of beautiful gypsy wagons. These were intricate and time consuming. Others did needlework, cross stitch and tapestry and some adapted their prison issue clothing, designing badges or making hats from the bottom of trouser legs or vests out of t-shirts. Some used their talents to design and create weapons, I have described some earlier. Knuckle dusters had been created and the cleverest thing I saw was the tattoo guns which had been fashioned from the inside parts of a radio cassette player. The cog wheel had been used to create the up and down action like a miniature sewing machine needle to create a tattoo.

The creation of homemade tattoos has diminished considerably in the thirteen years I worked at the prison, probably due to the fact that people are becoming more aware of the risks involved of contracting a blood borne virus such as Hepatitis C or HIV. The prisoners would also get 'nicked' and be up for adjudication, a punishment, which could result in loss of privileges, time in the segregation unit or further days added to their sentence, depending on the severity of the behaviour, if they were caught. We would only find out about these illicit tattoos when they had gone wrong and become infected wounds and we would need to become involved in the dressing of them or prescribing some antibiotics. I cannot remember the last time I saw one.

The other weapons used more frequently when we had the young offender population were simple tins of tuna or snooker balls put into socks and swung at the victim and made very effective weapons. Chair legs and snooker cues and metal crutches would also be used. They were extremely volatile at times and violence was high. Frequent calls were made to healthcare to attend to injuries caused from fighting. The worst injuries were the burns made from boiled sugar water which not only scalded the skin but would stick like glue and be extremely difficult to get off. When cold water was applied to cool the skin, it would harden. These cause extensive scarring.

One of the most superior weapons made was a full-size crossbow which was made with the matchsticks and glue which was easily obtainable because it was classed as crafting and provided to them for hobby making. They were allowed to keep this in their cells. When the crossbow was discovered, the prisoner was taken to the seg. It could have caused serious injury to another person; it was strong and fully functional. The officers took it out into the yard and were firing pencils out of it and it had a good range. The prisoner's story was that he had made it for his son.

Another ingenious item was a walking cane made from the matchstick and glue materials. This combined was very strong. They had encased a normal lightweight walking stick in the matchsticks and left a hole in the hollow to transport drugs/ medication in. They had disguised this by having a top piece which fitted on like a cap but was difficult to see the joining piece, again, very ingenious.

I saw tablets moulded individually from blu tak and then painted white and others fashioned from minute pieces of S -shaped packing foam. These would be used to replace the number of actual tablets or capsules which they had traded from their medication pots to others. I was always one step ahead of them though and had learnt to never trust face value the appearance of the medications they were willingly showing me when I performed a medication check, but to be vigilant when checking. They would take the capsules apart and trade the powder contents to others and either replace them in the packets or pots empty or replace the contents with talcum powder or even laundry detergent powder. They definitely had too much time on their hands to be able to do this and a lot of patience. We were robust, and if caught we would carry out the threats and warnings issued of stopping their medication, either tapering it down gradually on a reduction plan or stopping it immediately. It was clear they had not been taking it themselves and therefore that they did not need it.

Manipulation

I had a young guy on my caseload who was receiving prescribed methadone for substance misuse addiction and had been for many months, he was in his late twenties and had served 10 years over his tariff. This means he should have been released ten years earlier but due to his poor behaviour during his sentence he had kept having his parole refused or 'knocked back' as they describe it. He had been in prison since age 18. He was a cheeky chap and had the gift of the gab, a typical Essex boy, and chatted incessantly every morning when he attended healthcare to receive his see to take medications. He was always bright and chirpy and generally always polite to us nurses.

At the time the prisoners were still smoking tobacco. I think half of the chatting was used to distract us from being vigilant in our checking of him. He was under surveillance by the officers due to them having received intelligence reports regarding him and there was a high suspicion of him trading medications. He took the methadone he was administered and swallowed it then opened his mouth to show it was empty.

He then was given his Pregabalin capsule, he took the water and again swallowed it, opened his mouth, when asked and I saw the red of the capsule up between his top gum cheek. He was attempting to conceal it and had pushed it back quickly when given it to hide it and keep it for trading. I challenged him and he then immediately took more water and did swallow it this time. When he opened his mouth again, he pulled his cheeks back with both fingers to show me the cheek cavities and prove he had indeed swallowed it, but of course he had already been caught attempting to divert it.

The officer, who was in the room stepped in and told him to empty his pockets. They were not supposed to carry anything over to healthcare when coming for their morning meds, because they can pass things to each other. The officer found his tobacco pouch in his pocket and opened it to reveal another six Pregabalin capsules, which he had clearly diverted and saved up to trade with. We had caught him out.

We then followed the protocols, and he was started on a reduction of his Pregabalin. He was also nicked by the prison. He tried everything in the book to get put back on that prescription and was determined, I'll give him that. He tried the mental health route, claiming he was prescribed it for anxiety, he may well have been , but luckily at the time we had a robust psychiatrist who did see him but offered him an alternative medicine, which he claimed didn't work for him and that was the only one, so he refused to have it.

He booked doctor's appointments to try and get it back on prescription, firstly he said he had nerve pain caused by falling and hurting his back many years previously but there was no medical evidence of MRI scans performed, or records of his injuries he claimed to have sustained. I recall some of the stories he told of him having been in a car accident, also of being pushed off a train when he was a child and falling over when tackled playing football. He was offered appointments with the physiotherapist but refused saying he had already tried this. We telephoned the gym and received confirmation that he was a regular attender and did weight training several times a day and looked physically fit and was in good shape.

He then tried to claim he was prescribed it to treat his epilepsy, also no witnessed fits were documented in his records and no diagnosis was recorded to show he had epilepsy. He had never been referred or seen by a neurologist. He was asked if he would like to be referred for this to have an assessment undertaken, but of course he also refused this.

He was drawing blanks in his attempt to get the Pregabalin back on prescription. His next step was to up the ante.

I received a telephone call over the weekend when we worked with only three staff on in healthcare, a minimum of two nurses, the third could be a healthcare assistant or a nurse. The wing officer had rung to say that the prisoner had cut his eyebrow and was bleeding and claiming he had had a fit in his cell. Bearing in mind, we did not run clinics on weekends and only were staffed to cope with emergencies and those that were absolutely necessary to see that day. We still had to finish administering the medications and visit the seg unit and had other duties which were necessary to undertake.

We had already seen him that morning and administered his methadone and there were no apparent injuries when we had seen him 2 hours earlier. After ascertaining that he was not in immediate danger or needing medical attention, I advised the officer not to send him over to healthcare but that we would get to him when we started our rounds of visiting the cells. He had also called the officers to his cell, when he reported his alleged fit and injury. The officer confirmed that he appeared to look fine and was not displaying any signs of affected level of consciousness or behaviour, in fact he was shouting and demanding to be let out of his cell, and off the wing to go to healthcare.

When we did arrive on the wing at his cell, the door was unlocked and he came to the door and looked shocked as he was not expecting us to be there. He thought the officer was unlocking him to take him to healthcare. He had wedged a piece of a matchstick into his cut to keep the wound open and stop it from sticking together. It did not need glueing or even a dressing other than a plaster. We found out later he had paid another prisoner to punch him to cause the injury, so he could say he had had a fit. Two days later his bruising started to come out and he did have black eyes from the punch he had received. He was likely in debt for the Pregabalin he had been trading with, that he had had confiscated.

He had been caught out and was angry so he then started shouting and threatening us and he said he would throw himself down the stairs to show us and that we would have to give him his Pregabalin back because he would need it for pain. We just advised him that this was not a good idea and that he just needed to accept that he would not get it re-prescribed.

Another stunt he pulled was when trying again with another doctor to persuade her to re-prescribe the Pregabalin, he claimed his Nan had died and he couldn't sleep and was suffering with anxiety. When the doctor checked his records, it turns out he had previously received some sleeping tablets but also that his Nan had already died twice before on other occasions. The doctor suggested he may benefit by talking to the mental health team again. It just shows how important it is to check the patients records thoroughly and not to trust that what they are telling you because they can certainly fabricate stories and manipulate you if they can get away with it.

The consultation was not going the way he wanted, so he leapt up out of his seat and grabbed a box of medication which was on the doctor's desk, which in all fairness should definitely not have been left on there. He then proceeded to take as many as he could, cramming them into his mouth as fast as he could. The doctor pressed the general alarm bell in the room and was almost instantly assisted by the officer who was stationed in healthcare outside the door, during the clinic sessions. Then, shortly afterwards they were joined by other officers who would run to the location, to assist in any emergency situation, when there was a general alarm. They pinned him down and restrained him, while he was still trying to swallow the tablets.

The tablets had been brought to the doctor prior to the consultation by an officer who had come back from an escort, where he had taken a prisoner to hospital for an appointment, and they had discharged him with codeine medication for pain relief. He had checked with the doctor whether the prisoner was allowed to take this back to the wing with him and keep it as an 'in possession' medication or not. The answer was no, and that's how it ended up on her desk. Yes, it should have been out of sight and been disposed of. She would have been planning on doing so and of course that would have been documented, but the interruption to her clinic time would have caused a delay.

We were always striving to keep to the allocated appointment times to allow all the patients to be seen during clinic sessions, as they were constrained with time restrictions to keep sessions within the prison's daily routine.

So, because our young man was still on a prescription of methadone and had swallowed several of the codeine tablets in addition to his methadone he had taken that morning, he was now at risk of an opiate overdose. This can lead to respiratory distress, respiratory failure and then cardiac arrest and death. He then needed to go out to hospital for possible opiate overdose treatment of Naloxone, which is the antidote medication and at the very least for monitoring and observation.

He was not popular with the security department that day. We had to call an ambulance because if they had taken him in a taxi, it would have been quicker, but he could have deteriorated on the way and the officers were not trained to deal with that. So off he went with two escorting officers to hospital. The prison orderly officer had to arrange the paperwork, handcuffs and chains and now rearrange the officer's duties because 2 staff out were now out of the rotation whilst attending the hospital. If that wasn't manipulation, I don't know what is?

Eventually he calmed down and accepted that he was not going to get his Pregabalin prescription back. He was definitely less chatty and cocky when he came in the mornings for his methadone. After several months or a year, I cannot remember the exact timing whilst attending his substance misuse 13-week review, he actually asked if he could start reducing down to come off his methadone.

I held 13-week reviews consultations with all the patients on my caseload for substance misuse. These were held with the patient, myself, a GP with substance misuse experience and a member of the substance misuse psycho-social team. This would be the patient's case worker. This was to catch up with how they were doing, to see if they felt they wanted to start reduction plans for coming off their methadone. They usually came in with a fighting head on and sat holding onto or gripping the arms of the chair whilst they gave their reasons of why they possibly couldn't go on a reduction.

I was quite surprised when he requested to start a reduction of his methadone prescription, but also it was not unusual when I heard his reason why. He was an IPP prisoner, serving an indeterminate prison sentence with no release date, but he had been notified of his next parole hearing and the only chance of getting a transfer to a Cat D prison or release would be if he could be off the methadone prescription, and clean for a substantial period of time. Cat D prisons generally do not accept prisoners who are still receiving a prescription of Methadone. They should have had plenty of time during their sentence to have come off it and be making as much effort as possible to be rehabilitated to reduce the chances of them reoffending when they get a release date and need to reintegrate back into society.

We came to an agreed plan, and he started his reduction. He was scared of course but we took it slowly and as they do; he began to gain confidence that he was ok and that he could do it and that he would survive and manage without the methadone. They become so dependent on it psychologically that their self-confidence and self-esteem need to be built back up.

He did very well and managed to come off the prescription. All went noticeably quiet as far as seeing him in healthcare after that for many months. In fact, I thought he had probably been moved and transferred to another prison. Then I received an application for an appointment to see him. He wanted a letter from me for the parole board to prove he had come off the methadone and stating he was no longer dependent on it and proof that he was clean. This involved him having regular urine drug screening and his attendance reports from the substance misuse team to show he had put in and done the work involved around substance misuse to help prevent relapse when he was released and reduce the risk of reoffending.

Of course I did the letter for him for the parole board. I then saw him again after he had received the news that he had been granted release. He was grinning from ear to ear and was so happy. He was also nervous because he didn't want to mess it up, but he also apologised to me for his past behaviours and thanked me for 'being tough' on him, and told me, 'You're the best, Miss, and that was what he had needed '. It was so nice to hear this from him, because it made it all worthwhile. I won't lie, it is a hard job, and hard being the bad guy. It is what they need and does not do anyone any favours allowing bad behaviours to go unnoticed with no repercussions. I think I am old school in my way of thinking, but I truly believe that these men needed rules and direction, and we were there to ensure this happened. It didn't mean I didn't care when I was appearing to be tough, and yes it did affect me. I would go home and question myself and my actions, but I also had the assurances and back up of my colleagues when we had a strong team to support me. The decisions were not all made entirely by me.

Special treatment

Another form of manipulation was when the prisoners were trying to get special treatment by using their self-perceived superiority and trying to smooth talk their way into getting you to agree to do what they wanted. This is a form of grooming, and these types of people are dangerous, and this is why they have ended up serving custodial sentences. They are professional groomers, and this is indeed a form of manipulation. Grooming is when a person builds up a relationship with a child, young person or a vulnerable adult who is at risk. The special treatment could be that they wanted to jump the queue and get an appointment with the healthcare team quicker than the normal waiting time or that they wanted to be referred to hospital or obtain treatment that they believed they were entitled to.

One man was local to the prison and was serving a sentence for molestation of young boys. He had been a recognised and trusted member of the local community and had been providing them private music tuition in his home. I saw him in a clinic one day. Not far into the consultation he let me know he knew who my in laws were, who lived in the village he was from and told me he knew my husband.

We did not disclose any personal information to patients as it could be used against you as blackmail if they wanted to try and manipulate you into bringing things in for them , trafficking banned articles or getting them special treatment, and asking that Healthcare informed the wing that they required extra mattresses, heaters, fans and sometimes a microwave for their cell or to advise they weren't suitable for certain types of employment or that they needed extra gym sessions or whatever they wanted to try and obtain.

I had nothing to hide from him and quickly turned it around, agreeing with him, saying yes that's who they are and asked him if I should say hello to them from him? Of course that is not what he was expecting or how the conversation he had started was supposed to go, because he quickly backtracked as it would have been obvious that I had seen him in prison and he likely wanted the minimalistic amount of attention or people to know about his crime or that he was currently serving a sentence.

We had another prisoner a high-profile man who had been a celebrity publicist and was serving a sentence for indecent assaults and rape of women. Because he was high profile, he expected special treatment and portrayed himself as being very important and that we had a duty to allow him priority care. The governors did not help with this as they seemed very concerned about ensuring his hearing aids were ordered in as quickly as possible and that we chased them up to make sure he didn't have to wait a long time for them. He was an NHS patient along with the other 1200 patients we had in our care. At the end of the day, he was treated the same by us in healthcare and he should not have received priority care just because he was high profile. He had committed crimes and was serving a sentence for them the same as all of the others.

He asked me if I thought the governor would allow him to have a swimming pool built in the prison as he was missing his daily swimming exercise. He told me that of course he would allow all of the nurses to use it. I advised him that I thought it highly unlikely that that this would be approved or would be allowed. I didn't add in that I certainly would not actually want to swim in the pool that they were swimming in, or that I wasn't impressed with the fact that he was offering to pay for it because it felt like he was just gloating about having the money to afford it and was likely trying to just get my attention to treating him with more respect for who he was and for his esteem. I was treating him the same as the other patients and without any special preference. I certainly did not buy into his beliefs of his own self-importance.

Inappropriate Relationships

During my time working there, there had been various inappropriate relationships between staff and prisoners, which really baffled me. It has happened a lot across a lot of prisons nationally and I really don't understand the thinking behind this of a staff member risking their job to have an affair with a prisoner. One of these involved a healthcare assistant whose parents were both also employed by the prison and she had been having a relationship with a prisoner. She had been caught out and had been putting notes to arrange their meeting times into packets of paracetamol and taking them down to the wing for him. She had passed one of these notes to the cleaner who cleaned the corridors outside healthcare, and he had eventually reported it.

Another was a drug support worker again having been having relations with a prisoner, she had been caught and had been having sex with him in an office. A female mental health support worker had been seeing a prison officer and was then two-timing him with a prisoner. Imagine how the poor officer felt. Luckily all of these had been caught and sacked from their jobs and in all honesty, it served them right.

There were also officers who had been involved with prisoners and been caught bringing in items for them. One male officer had been doing this and was actually having a relationship with the prisoner's wife, who after losing his job he continued to have a relationship with her.

Some officers were having affairs with other officers whilst married but this wasn't unheard of or a crime. Officers having affairs with prisoners can end up serving a sentence.

The Dangers of co-prescribing.

I am a Non-Medical Prescriber and I along with other nurses, pharmacists and any health professionals who have worked extremely hard to achieve this qualification know that we are as accountable for our prescriptions as all the doctors were accountable for theirs. It is your name on the prescription and therefore if any incidents occur involving the prescribed medications, investigations will follow.

The young man mentioned who was caught concealing his Pregabalin in his tobacco pouch was on a combination of Methadone and Pregabalin. This can be a dangerous combination of drugs, but many were on these medications co-prescribed. We had started to review the medications and were trying to stop these prescriptions and change to alternatives to keep patients safer and reduce the risk of harm. This was to ensure we were keeping in line with the NICE guidance on opiate prescribing, dependence forming medications, substance misuse and pain management.

The combination of these two drugs can cause respiratory depression which can lead to respiratory failure and cause death in the extreme, and likely would if someone who wasn't used to this, took it. Patients that were already established on this combination would have had the dose titrated up gradually over a period of time when the second medication was introduced so they were able to tolerate it. However, it is not recommended, and we were working our way through the high numbers to try and keep our prescribing safe and follow the guidelines.

Pregabalin is an interesting drug and when it came out it was a new 'wonder drug 'it was being prescribed to patients to treat anxiety, epilepsy and nerve pain. What wasn't known or mentioned when it was brought onto the market was that it is an addictive medication with dependence forming properties and difficult for people to wean themselves off, especially those who suffer with anxiety anyway. We had to trawl back through patient's records to find the reason for the prescription choice and look at who had prescribed it and when.

In prisons it is highly tradeable and even back 10 years ago its value in the prison was higher than in the community because it is more scarcely available. It was worth around £8 a tablet. It comes in a capsule form, and they used to break open the capsule and snort the powder, this would give a euphoric effect, and they loved it. It wasn't always kept securely and administered as a controlled drug and recorded in the Controlled Drugs (CD) Register but that was put into practice by our wonderful pharmacist and became the practice of all the other prisons under the trust because it was highly sought after, and because it could cause harm.

The other drug the prisoners loved to get their hands on was Buprenorphine or Subutex, its trade name. We had barely any patients on this for substitute opiate treatment, and this was kept in the CD register. When we administered it, we had to crush it first and check the patients mouth was empty and ask them to drink some water first, sometimes they could put clear plastic in the back of the throat to catch it but more often they would try and wedge chunks or pieces of a tablet into their dental cavities in their teeth. The crushed subutex was then tipped under the front of the tongue to dissolve.

One day, one of the patients right in front of my eyes, took the pot of powder from me, tipped it onto the counter, bent down and snorted it up into his nostril, so fast I couldn't do anything neither could the officer who also witnessed it. We couldn't believe it! He then just looked up and laughed at us all! Of course that earned him a trip straight down to the Seg. He also received a nicking and had to stay down there a while and lost his privileges, TV, association time and canteen items, but he must have thought doing his little trick was worth it!

We are no longer allowed to use the term, manipulative behaviour when referring to prisoners who are basically trying to bend and break the rules. The trust I was working for was essentially using a mental health model which was brought into play during my latter years of my employment with them. They brought in the term, 'trauma informed' which meant we had to show more understanding and compassion for the patients who had come from very disturbed traumatic backgrounds, and I really and truly get this and understand it. What I had a difficult time with was that of when someone had clearly been caught out, diverting their medications, and been issued with a written warning and informed that their medication would be stopped, if they got caught again, and of course they did. Then we would, as a multidisciplinary team discuss the case and agree on a plan of reduction or immediate stopping of the medication if safe to do so.

We had clearly written procedures, protocols and policies in place for this as it happened so regularly. These policies had been ratified at a higher clinical governance level within the trust, not just locally to our practice and they were there to show a clear structure of proceedings to be followed. The problem I had, was when this had happened and the patient had received their letter informing them of the decision and plan to stop the medication, the Mental Health nursing team would get the patient complaining to them and claiming it was affecting their mental health, it wasn't fair, they couldn't possibly manage without them etc, etc. The mental health nurses would try and advocate for the patient and give their best to helping the patient, as it is in all our natures as nurses to do this. They would go against the policies in place and persuade the psychiatrist at the time to re-start the exact same medication. We were going round in circles at times.

Now I did not have a problem of them being switched onto another medication to treat their conditions if it was necessary, but they should have provided an alternative medication that was not considered to be a tradeable medication. That would have been the ideal way to deal with this. It would also have not caused angst and frustration within our nursing healthcare team of general nursing and mental health nurses as we should have been working succinctly. There was still at times a divide between the, them and us which was more apparent when under the prison service because the mental health team had been working for another trust , but when the TUPE (Transfer of Undertakings (Protection of Employment) happened we were one integrated team all employed by the same trust to provide joined up patient care.

We did have some robust psychiatrists and doctors at times which worked very well, and by communicating regularly and discussing certain patients it could work very effectively. The problems occurred when we had scarcely any time with the psychiatrists who only came in one day a week and were so busy catching up with the whole caseload of patients and running clinics throughout the day, there was little time to have a meeting to discuss these cases.

Pain Management

We had developed an excellent pain management pathway, and this was also to explore and create a way of reviewing the medications that were tradeable and could potentially cause harm when taken by others it was not prescribed for. These medications included those known as dependence forming medications and included the stronger pain relievers, and opiate based medications. We are also expected to follow National guidelines when prescribing and in more recent years the National Institute of Clinical Excellence (NICE) guidelines have produced new and updated guidelines for managing chronic pain and opioid use.

We set up the group initially when we had some very motivated robust doctors who came in when we were taken over by the trust, they all knew each other and had worked in the same practice in the community. They were awesome, and just what we needed, they brought in new ideas, and ways of working to our practice. It was backed up with the production of documented guidance in the form of policies, protocols and procedures. This provided us with protection when the complaints from the prisoners started to came in. It was developed with a structured approach and framework. It was proactive and they led us forward, and suddenly we had structure and leadership and organisation, and a real team bonding occurred. We felt more motivated and supported than we had ever before. This was all at the time of us being transferred across from the prison service employment to the NHS trust employment which enabled us to gain the stability of having a contract with this new group of doctors as a pose to the previous provision of General Practitioner doctors (GP's). TUPEd. At this time also we set up Clinical Governance within the healthcare and initially this was started with local in-house meetings,

It then expanded over the next nine years as the trust expanded. The trust bid for and won contracts and took on more and more prisons, detention centres, immigration centres and youth custody centres. We then, as managers travelled monthly to the expanded Clinical Governance meetings to discuss and share practices to improve ways of working and become united across all sites within the trust in the provision of patient care.

Sadly, the excellent doctors we had been privileged to have had working alongside us all gradually left to retire or reduce their workloads after a few years, but when they initially came in, and the changes happened, it was an excellent place to work.

The lead doctor at the time encouraged me to attend several conferences on pain management with her and I learnt so much, it was refreshing and that's when the multidisciplinary team was set up for Medicines Management and Pain Management clinics, all this integrated very well with my role as the Clinical Substance Misuse Manager. I was also the Drug Strategy Lead and link with the Prison Service and attended the monthly prison Security meetings to discuss drugs and substance misuse.

The multidisciplinary team consisted of the lead doctor, who also at the time was lead for substance misuse and the lead doctor in pain management, myself, the Pharmacist manager, and the physiotherapist. We audited the prescribed medications for pain management, reviewed the patient's history, looked at previous interventions, actual diagnosis they had and whether these were proven. Then we looked at treatments they had received in addition to medication, such as physiotherapy. Alongside this we checked histories of abuse of medications, including compliance and looked at any documented records of them having been caught diverting or of bullying.

Some of the information I would bring to the meeting from the security meeting I attended which was that of the prison suspecting them to be dealing or trading their own and other medications. Suspicious behaviours included the transfer of money into and outside of their accounts, and conversations listened to by the prison staff to gain information about illicit drugs. and of them attempting to get them in along with mobile phones so they could arrange deals, smuggling items in with visitors, sent in the post as they sprayed the synthetic substances such as spice onto paper which could be disguised as a painting or a picture drawn by their child and be covered in the substance which when torn into tiny pieces could be worth several thousand pounds!

Attempted Escapes

We didn't have many attempted escapes from the prison and there had been only one successful one many years before I was there when a prisoner had got out by climbing and throwing himself over the extremely high perimeter fencing and made it almost to the nearest dual carriageway of a major A road, he was covered in blood and his clothes were shredded from the razor blade wiring which is coiled at the top of the fencing.

Another had attempted to escape under the bread lorry that came in with supplies of bread to the kitchens. A full paramedic ambulance uniform was found in someone's cell with the badges sewn on by hand in an attempt for someone to try and get out on one of the ambulances that regularly came in. Why they thought they would go undetected with an ambulance crew who would obviously know he wasn't one of their crew, ceases to amaze me, unless the plan was to take them hostage in order to get him out. Also, someone had made a ladder by collecting pieces of wood from the recycling bins and carpentry workshops over a period of time and then tied them together with strips of bedsheets. Luckily this was found before being put to use.

We had nothing as exciting as the escape which happened from a London prison where someone had managed to fly in an angle grinder on a drone and had cut the bars off the cell window and enabled a prisoner to escape.

Illicit items

The perimeter fencing was checked on a twice daily basis to search for illicit items which were known as 'throw overs'. Drugs could be thrown over as well as any illicit items such as mobile phones/ weapons by putting them inside dead ducks, pigeons, rats or rabbits as we were in a rural location, so any dead animals had to be checked. Inner city prisons would be more likely to have medications or drugs thrown over inside tennis balls or even attached to coins especially if there was netting in place in the outside yards used as a ceiling to try and prevent this from happening.

As drones started to become popular, they could also be used as a means of transportation of illicit items.

Then there were visitors who attempted to traffic in illicit items and sadly sometimes the staff, both prison and non-prison employed.

Mobiles had been brought in inside plastic bags which had been put inside milk cartons in the milk. Visitors have been caught smuggling in drugs and passing them to their prisoners in the visits hall, sometimes hidden in the heel of their shoes. We had sniffer dogs and visitors would receive a full rub down search. We had no X-ray machines or wands as it was a Category C prison, but at the Cat B and A prisons this was in place. The latest method used for smuggling in 'spice, was by spraying it onto paper. This was in books, reading books which were sent or brought in, on pictures they had sent in drawn by their children to disguise it or even on legal documents and papers. We even had to resort to photocopying of all of these paper items to deter and stop this happening as we didn't have a scanner to put all the paper through to test it.

Drugs had also been found hidden inside one of the older prisoners walking sticks and a syringe with a needle inside a pen, which had had the inside removed and been replaced with the syringe.

Other items classed as contraband, aside from the usual weapons, tools and drugs that you are not allowed to take inside the prison were alcohol, tinfoil, blu tack, paperclips, staples, chewing gum, tobacco and lighters or matches. Any pornographic material is also banned.

Tinfoil could be used to cook up drugs on , clingfilm to try and divert drugs, some could put a piece of clear plastic in the back of their throat and trap the tablets in their oesophagus so it would look like it had been swallowed when they had their mouths checked. They must have had no gag reflex to be able to do this. The paper clips and staples could be used as a needle when creating tattoos or used to pick locks. The lighters, matches and tobacco were made contraband when the prisons were all made smoke free and there were also some prisoners, who were serving sentences for arson. Blu tack and chewing gum can be used to gum up the locks on cell doors or to make impressions of the officers keys.

Another item you would probably not even think about that wasn't allowed to be taken in was metal cutlery. This could easily be used as a weapon. So, we had to make use of plastic cutlery to eat our lunches with. We had ceramic mugs in healthcare and throughout the prison, the officers and other admin staff used them, but there were plenty found in prisoners cells, which had been 'obtained'. The prison issued regulation mugs and plates and bowls were made of plastic. As I mentioned earlier the ceramic mugs had been used to smash across people's heads.

Patients

We had an elderly patient who reminded me of 'Shergar' the racehorse, because of his teeth, which were too big for his mouth and in order to keep them in and stop them from slipping; he always looked like he had a permanent grin on his face. I was out on the wings one afternoon seeing other patients, when I was approached by an officer who asked me if I could check on this man because he was covered in urine. I knew the patient and he had a long-term urinary catheter in situ which had been by-passing, this means it had become blocked, and the urine was now leaking around the tube it was supposed to flow through and caused him to be incontinent of urine. His clothing was wet and soaked in urine, this had caused his skin to become excoriated and burnt and very sore from the urine. He also had an inguinal hernia the size of a rugby ball in his scrotum.

There was a character called 'Buster Gonad' in a comic, which was around in the 1980's called 'Viz' who used to push his testicles around in a wheelbarrow and this poor little man who was 83 years old and had already suffered from four heart attacks in the past and had multiple co-morbidities had been told that he couldn't have his hernia operated on to reduce its size and make him more comfortable because the risk of surgery would be too great to risk him having an anaesthetic. So, he had to endure this debilitating quality of life. He was brought over to healthcare in a wheelchair and we re-catheterised him and treated his burnt skin. Despite his problems, he always was very grateful and remained cheerful. He always appeared to be smiling, but then again, it could have been attributed to those large dentures!

When we were placing the new catheter, we always used a chaperone as it was an intimate procedure. Due to the man's age and the fact he had the large inguinal hernia in his groin, let's just say he wasn't the easiest patient to place a new catheter into. I was trying to locate the urethra and even find his penis which had retracted under many folds of skin, and I was having a job to find it! So I had to do a fair bit of digging around and had to keep checking with him that he was ok and it was not too uncomfortable for him, because of his large teeth he appeared to be grinning at me the whole time and saying, 'oh, no dear, it's not hurting me, you carry on !' I couldn't tell but it appeared to be that he was actually quite enjoying all of the attention. I am pleased to say we did manage to successfully complete the procedure in the end.

Love Letter

One morning, whilst sat in my office, I heard a chuckling from my colleague, who had the office opposite mine and we were friends, 'what are you laughing at?' I asked her, she said, 'oh dear , this has made me laugh', one of the transgender prisoners, (I'll call her Ruby to keep her anonymous) has taken the utmost offence to a letter she's received which has been pushed under her cell door by an admirer and she's gone flouncing up to the office and handed it in to the officers feeling most upset and undignified!' Ruby is declaring that it is 'out of order' and 'how dare they', now bearing in mind that Ruby dresses up to the nines with a very flirtatious look about her and dresses provocatively in short skirts, high heels, a lot of makeup and a long blonde wig she is giving out the impression that she is 'on the game, so to speak', myself and my friend, said she should be flattered with the attention!

The love letter said,' I love your voluptuous body and the way you swing your hips and swish your hair; I love the way you walk; I love your legs and thighs. I want to come to your cell at night and I want to smash your back doors in, so you won't be able to walk for a week, when I'm finished with you. I know you might think that I am a predator, and I am, but that's what predators do.'

The funny part that tickled my colleague was the reaction that came from the officers who had read the letter and one was studiously writing some of the contents down and they were saying that they would use some of the phrases in their valentine's day cards to their wives and partners if it was going to cause such a response and a reaction, the fact she found it to be offensive was not really considered by them but it tickled their fancy.

The officers would have had to report this information to the Security department as intelligence and it would then trigger an investigation into discovering who the perpetrator was in order that they could receive an adjudication, or negative behaviour report or warning against their record and of course that would also depend on whether or not and how far Ruby wanted to pursue the event and take action and how threatened she felt as a consequence of the action. She may have and quite likely did enjoy the attention that this had caused, and by reporting the incident to wider parties by involving the officers, she gained more attention from it. Of course, she could have chosen to have kept this private and to herself and shown no reaction which is often the best action as it causes the perpetrator to cease their attentions, get bored and move onto someone else.

Another incident involving an elderly prisoner, who was sentenced at the age of 84 years old for a historic crime from 40 years previously, arrived in the prison and was very well spoken and had been a headmaster in a private boarding school for many years. He had the attitude that he could buy his way through his sentence and always informed everybody about his wealth. I remember him discussing his private cardiac consultation he had been having on a yearly basis and asking if I could arrange the appointment for me. I had to remind him that he was in prison now and that he was unable to have this arranged and he would have to wait for a referral through the NHS and within the normal waiting times and he would be added to a list. He was adamant that no he could afford to pay for a private taxi and appointment with his consultant. Unfortunately, no, he couldn't do this as he had now lost his rights to his liberty to do this.

The underlying reason for me writing this is about his arrogance around displaying his wealth, he told everybody about it. So, after he was released after serving 30 months, another prisoner, a 55-year-old convicted double killer, who was out on day release from prison, turned up at his house unannounced under the pretext of seeking help in setting up a charity to support elderly ex-offenders. He entered the elderly man's house and tied him up to his bed, stuffed the silver family heirlooms into a pillowcase and demanded his bank card and PIN numbers from him. He was screaming for his life. I think his arrogance left him then. Unfortunately, his 66-year-old neighbour heard the screaming coming from the house and ran around to help the elderly man and ended up having his throat slashed wide open and died on the front lawn with his dog sitting beside him.

The prisoner ran off and was rearrested several days later from being spotted on a CCTV camera. He is now serving a further 40-year sentence following the previous two sentences of ten years for manslaughter for which he served eight and then received twenty-five years for murder. He will not be released now for a very long time, if ever. He has obviously not been rehabilitated or learnt from being incarcerated for many years.

We also have had some prestigious people who have been sentenced and believe they deserve better treatment and display arrogance in their behaviour when they think they can pay for extra privileges and believe that they are better than others. The same high profile man that asked if I thought the governor would agree to him paying to have a swimming pool built within the prison, was serving eight years for historic offences and died in prison of natural causes caused by a rare condition in his heart leading him to have congestive cardiac failure.

This condition was diagnosed whilst he was in prison and would have led to his death wherever he was, in prison or at home, but his family blame the prison and healthcare for his death, stating if he had received better conditions of living, improved comfort and treatment then he would not have died. This is totally misunderstood, and I understand it is extremely difficult to accept a death of a family member especially when you have been shamed because they are in prison and people want to apportion blame to help themselves deal with it and to cope and to accept death. This is a process that some people have to go through to enable them to accept the death of their relative, partner or friend.

Deaths in Custody

We as nurses learn to cope well and manage to deal with death throughout our careers and I am so grateful to the nursing team I worked with for the support we gave to each other on a daily basis, I truly appreciated and loved them as my work family as they were always there for me and I was for them when we were having a bad day, needed a hug, or a bit of support or an ear to just listen to enable us to offload if we need to.

As coping with death goes, it is always easier to accept when you have an expected death which goes hand in hand with long term illnesses. You have time to prepare for it, and plans can be made, making acceptance easier. Although, having said that we had two long drawn-out deaths which were self-inflicted as both the men were refusing food and were slowly starving themselves to death and both succeeded.

Food Refusal

I do not believe the first man was classed as being on a hunger strike as what he had started as an intentional weight loss, had become out of hand and uncontrolled with him having had mental health issues. A hunger strike is usually done in order to gain some control of a situation or as a protest to something a person does not agree with and doesn't generally last long term.

The first man to die from starvation caused from food refusal was extremely difficult to accept from a health professional's perspective as we are here to provide care and help in getting people better. He was in his forties and was serving an IPP sentence. He had been very violent to his wife and raped her and beaten her badly several times. He was originally from a traveller community and used illicit substances and drugs and lost control. Despite all of that she had forgiven him and did used to visit. When he had arrived as a transfer from another prison he was in a state and in withdrawal from having been using illicit substances at the last prison. He arrived and within a few days I had received a request for him to see me for help. He had been using opiate medication he had obtained from other prisoners and had become addicted to Tramadol. He was also on a prescription of the maximum dose of Pregabalin which when taken in combination with an opiate caused an enhanced effect of the opiate.

I assessed him and we agreed on a plan of a methadone prescription which would prevent him from going into withdrawal and he would be expected to work with the substance misuse team workers to help his psychosocial aspects and for him to address his issues and help with his anxiety. He also was a very tall heavily built man. I later assessed and diagnosed him with having Obstructive Sleep Apnoea and initiated him on a CPAP machine to help him to get good quality sleep. I knew him well and for several years.

After one of the visits from his wife and him receiving a date for his next parole hearing, he got enough motivation to start a reduction of his methadone prescription, and he successfully managed to come off his methadone. He always told me during our appointments that he suffered with anxiety and also had a diagnosis of emotionally unstable personality disorder and obsessive-compulsive disorder and that once he set his mind to something he would become compulsive about, it in achieving his goal.

During the COVID lockdown, at times, the prisoners ended up being locked in their cells for many more hours than the normal daily regime dictated. This was due to many prison officers who were the wing staff officers, being off sick with Covid. The officers and all staff working in the prison including us working in healthcare, had to be tested every morning upon arrival at the prison and before they went to their designated work areas. The wing officers had to swab test the prisoners, every morning of up to 60 people on the landings, and lock any down behind their doors for days at a time that had tested positive until they had 2 x clear swabs for 48 hr periods. In order to placate them and keep them quiet they would be given extra full sugar drinks, packets of crisps and biscuits every day.

We nurses and the pharmacy staff had to hand deliver the see to take medication to the individual cells during some of the lockdown when there were outbreaks and there was no movement allowed.

I could see this man getting heavier and heavier as the weeks and months went by, the exercise regimes were stopped and attendance at the gym so that didn't help either and he was also employed as a server on the wings, these men always got first helpings and extras of the hot food from the servery. So, after several months of lockdown, by this time he had gained an extra 3 stone in weight and was obese.

I don't know what triggered him to start dieting but he did and the weight loss was dramatic, once allowed back into the gym he went to as many sessions as he was allowed and was also exercising excessively in his cell with plastic bags wrapped around him under his clothes to increase the amount he sweated.

He had become obsessed with his weight loss and I remember him arriving in healthcare for one of his covid vaccinations wearing a vest and a woolly hat and he had lost so much weight by this time I hardly recognised him as the same man. He had lost over 5 stone in about 8 months, fat and muscle and was skeletal with very saggy skin. It was difficult to give the intramuscular injection into his upper arm for fear of hitting the bone. Once he had stopped his see to take Pregabalin medication he has stopped attending healthcare twice a day and gone under the radar so to speak, so it had gone unnoticed by the healthcare staff that he had lost so much weight. I was shocked, he also no longer needed to use the CPAP machine as he had cured his obstructive sleep apnoea by losing so much weight.

Everyone tried to convince him to eat, he was seen twice weekly by the nurses who would do his observations, recording his blood pressure, pulse, and weight, when he would allow us to. We also took his bloods, and he had several ECGs. (Electrocardiograms). He was seen by the mental health team, the mental health nurses the psychiatrist, and the psychologist. The prison was trying to arrange a transfer to a Category D open prison, but it was many miles north and far away from his family which for him, would mean very few visits from his wife as it was pretty much inaccessible using public transport. They also refused to accept him when they discovered his state of health. We were duty bound to disclose this and as it was in a remote setting, it would have been more difficult for them to get him to a hospital if the need arose.

The prison staff were extremely concerned about him and what they should do if he became unwell when healthcare were not on duty, but it was the same procedure to follow as for any unwell person needing medical attention and treatment when we were not in the establishment. They would telephone the out of hours service and could ring for an ambulance.

He was placed on an ACCT for many months, he was seen by the chaplain regularly, the safer custody team, his personal wing officers, and the Independent Monitoring Board, (IMB) these were voluntary members of the public, usually older retired people who would come into the prison in their free time and take up any concerns that had been raised by the prisoners. If they felt the prisoner needed an advocate to support them and to give them the empathy and autonomy to help them with their raised concerns and issues., then they would take up their case. They did mean well and did a great job, but it was also sometimes difficult for them to understand that actually we were not punishing the prisoners as the prisoners would lead them to believe. The prisoners would often miss out the truth and omit the major points in their history telling, for example, when they had been put onto a reduction of their medication that they had been caught diverting and were not actually taking it for themselves as prescribed.

The IMB person would turn up unannounced outside my office door on occasion with no preset time or arranged appointment made. I would then be expected to sit and explain the story and have to fill in the gaps and explain that, no, they would not be getting the medication back despite them claiming to need it. The IMB obviously did not have access to the patient's medical records as this would have been a breach of confidentiality, and although they wanted all the answers to their questions to be explained, it took up my time that sometimes I did not have the availability of.

Healthcare also tried to get him medically admitted to the nearest local hospital with a unit that catered for anorexia patients, but due to him serving a sentence for a sexual offence he was not accepted as it would have been inappropriate for him to have been placed onto a ward where these were filled usually full of young female patients, the majority of the time.

The other prisoners were also very concerned about him as well because they could see the gradual deterioration and it was frustrating to all that he was doing this to himself. Before he was taken out to hospital, the mental health team were trying to get him 'sectioned under the mental health act 'to enable him to be transferred to a psychiatric unit, where he would be taken against his will. This was done in his best interests, to see if he was deemed as being mentally unfit to make the decision to refuse to go out to a psychiatric unit.

He had an assessment undertaken to check whether he was lacking the mental capacity to make the decision. The decision was that he did indeed have full mental capacity and that he was not lacking capacity. A person can still have capacity if the decision made is not seen as a wise decision and when everyone else does not agree with that decision, it doesn't mean it is the wrong one, or that they are lacking in capacity. This was extremely difficult to accept because everyone could see him becoming worse each day.

After weeks and weeks of trying to persuade him to eat and giving him nutritional supplements in the form of protein drinks, he became less mobile with extreme muscle loss and had to be moved downstairs from the second landing and located flat on the ground floor. He was emaciated and skeletal by this point with a yellowish pasty colouring of his skin, which was now hanging off him in folds, his bones were sticking out, he had severe muscle wastage and weakness, and his legs could no longer fully support. He now had moved into a state of cachexia. He started to need care in his cell with his normal activities of daily living such as washing and dressing and with transferring into the wheelchair. He had become so weak he could no longer walk over to healthcare and ended up having to be pushed everywhere in the wheelchair.

He collapsed several times and fell in his cell, and he eventually was sent out to hospital and was nursed in Intensive care and despite being fed by tube he suffered several heart attacks and went into renal and multi organ failure and eventually died.

The second one to be on a food refusal was a man who had also arrived at the prison as a transfer in from another prison. He had recently received the news from his recent court hearing that his sentence had been set for a very long time. He had already been refusing food and was on a hunger strike at the sending prison because he was not accepting of his sentence, and he felt he no longer wanted to live.

He was very detached and unemotional when spoken to and when you were trying to persuade and encourage him to change his decision and to eat. He just appeared to be complacent, and apathetic about the whole situation. He stuck to his guns, and he also slowly deteriorated. Again, all the departments tried their best to try to tempt him round and encourage him to change his mind.

He had requested to have an advanced directive put in place which specified his wishes that he did not want any form of resuscitation performed under any circumstances. This is also known as a living will and allows you the opportunity to put your wishes into place about your death. It specifies the treatment you are willing to receive and also the treatment that you don't want to receive, such as any life sustaining treatment to be used to prevent you from dying. Or it can also state that you are willing to accept medications to help with pain symptoms or distress. He had a capacity assessment and was deemed to have full capacity. As mentioned earlier, capacity should be assumed unless there are serious reasons either temporary or permanent to lead you to believe otherwise. The mental capacity act has an impact on those who are not detained under the mental health act, and he was not and had not been sectioned.

He also become very emaciated and spent long hours in his cell, literally waiting to die, which he did. He had reached a cachexic state which is a complex metabolic syndrome and is also known as wasting syndrome of weight loss and causes muscle wasting and fat loss, weakness and lethargy and fatigue which cannot be reversed by simply consuming more calories. This is caused with intentional avoidance of food of a hunger strike. Healthcare received a call one morning as he had been found on his toilet in his cell and couldn't get himself off as he was so weak and had no strength left in his legs. I did not personally attend this code, but I know it was extremely difficult for my colleagues who did and that it affected them emotionally. One was a younger nurse who had previously worked in a busy accident and emergency department in a hospital and was primarily used to saving lives and treating people to help them recover from accidents and illness and because this man had the advanced directive in place which clearly stated he was refusing to be resuscitated They were unable to initiate and perform CPR and had to literally just be with him and watch and wait for him to die.

I think for me, although both deaths are hard to accept because we are there to nurse, I found the first man's death by far the hardest, due to having known him and looked after him for the few years that he was there for. He was always chatty and polite with me and was grateful for the help I had given him with his substance misuse issues. I just felt quite helpless that we weren't able to persuade him to change his mind.

The hardest deaths for people to deal with emotionally are those that are unexpected as you don't have that time to prepare yourself mentally for them. These include the successful suicides and those that had a sudden event that led to a death that could not be prepared for.

We had at least two successful hangings whilst I was there that I remember well but luckily for me I did not witness the dead bodies. This was the poor officers that had found them in their cells, and both had been dead for some time and were clearly deceased.

The first few years that I worked there, the prison policy stated that you had to start Cardiopulmonary Resuscitation, CPR. Even if the person is clearly dead, and showing no signs of life, is stone cold to the touch, and has marbled, and mottled skin and even if the body has become stiff indicating that rigor mortis has set in, I was told by a prison officer, they were still expected to start CPR and continue until the ambulance or a doctor arrived and advised them to stop. This is inappropriate and causes emotional trauma to those attempting to bring back life when there is clearly no chance of that happening. As an Advanced Nurse Practitioner, I was qualified to make this assessment and verify that death had occurred.

This happened one morning when we received a Code blue to a wing, and I attended with one of my colleagues who was a healthcare assistant. Upon arrival at the cell door which was already surrounded by all the wing officers and the duty governor, I saw the man was slumped over and lying on his left side on his bed. He was stone cold to the touch; his skin had a waxen yellowish appearance, and it had started to become mottled and had turned a deep reddish-purple colour and this had extended up to his head and face. It had taken on a marbled effect. His eyes were open and staring, his pupils were fixed with no response to light or stimuli, he had blood around his nostrils and was clearly dead with no response or signs of life. He had no carotid pulse or heart sounds when I listened with a stethoscope.

I completed the clinical assessment and checks whilst the officers were all cramming into the cell door and relaying the constant questions which were being sent over the radio net from the ambulance control via comms. I quickly told them to stand down the ambulance so that it wouldn't be sent as an emergency call as there was nothing they could do. As I came out of the cell the duty governor approached me in a bit of a frenzied state and asked me if the man had a DNAR status, a do not attempt resuscitation order, in place, to which I replied I didn't know. Without checking his medical notes, I could not verify this and that even if he did have one it was beyond being of any use now.

It was too late. The duty governor did not want to accept that we shouldn't be doing something more and as he was old school, he had also had the training that you have to attempt to resuscitate even when they are dead until the ambulance arrives. I repeated that it was too late and that it would be inappropriate and undignified to carry out CPR, but he still would not accept my decision or response. He then asked why I wouldn't start CPR and continue it until the ambulance arrived to verify the death. I accepted that he was trying to follow his procedures and was concerned that because the prison always have investigations carried out into every death in a custodial setting, he wanted to ensure that every possible attempt had been made to do the right thing.

His idea of the right thing and mine were different. I then had to become a bit blunter and more told him quite clearly that I was not starting CPR. That I was an Advanced Nurse Practitioner and more than capable and qualified to pronounce him as being dead. All of this was being recorded on the officers body worn cameras, and I remember one of the senior officers, who was standing behind the duty governor, hand signalling to me to indicate that the cameras were still recording the conversations. I have been known to be forthright in the past and he may have been concerned that I would get carried away with my language, so to speak and he was warning me to tone it down a bit.

Shortly after this conversation we heard on the radio that the ambulance had arrived at the prison and was in the gate and would soon be arriving at the wing. When the paramedics arrived on the wing and were shown over to where we were, I gave a handover of the circumstances to them. They then carried out their assessment of the man. The paramedic agreed with my decision and said I had absolutely done the correct thing and that he would have done the same and to have attempted to resuscitate would have been a futile exercise. This was very reassuring for me because when you are pressured and in a stressful situation, you need support and not the feeling that you are doing something wrong. It is harder to stand your ground when you are one individual nurse against a group of prison officers, senior officers and the duty governor and working in their establishment.

 Once the duty governor had a conversation with the paramedics who confirmed that I had dealt with the situation in the correct manner. He then seemed to visibly relax and accepted their explanation. This was slightly annoying from my point of view, not to have been believed but also it was a relief. I also had to be interviewed by the police and give a statement, which is all within the normal procedures which happen when there is a death in custody.

Hangings

The two deaths caused by hanging, were found in their cells, one had strung himself up from the bars in the window, he had hung himself in the night and had been dead for several hours before he was discovered. He was found stone cold in the morning, the officers had cut him down, they carry a tool on their belts known as a cut down knife or fish knife which is specifically used for this purpose. They did attempt to resuscitate him whilst waiting for the ambulance to arrive and because it was during the night, there were no healthcare staff on duty to call on to assist in the establishment because our working hours only covered from 07.30am until 19.30pm. The working hours are not always the same. Each prison has different contracts with healthcare and a lot of them run healthcare over 24hrs and 7 days a week. He had left a suicide note and had become very depressed and had just had enough with no hope of a future and of getting released.

The other man had hung himself from his door handle by tying the noose he had made from his bedsheets to the door handle on the inside of his cell door. He had successfully managed to do this over the lunch period. When the officers open the cell doors, they have to check whereabouts the prisoner is in the cell, by opening the door hatch. Sometimes the prisoner could be slightly out of full view if they were using the toilet or shower. If this is the case, then the officer shouts to try and get a response. When they didn't get one, the door was opened, but they were unable to push the door open due to the man's body blocking it, he was slumped forward in the sitting position and not breathing, but had only recently died, as he was still warm.

The officer sounded the alarm, and a code blue was put out on the radio. The nurses attended and attempted to resuscitate him with the assistance of the officers. I cannot remember clearly whether he was pronounced dead at the scene or whether he was intubated and transferred to the hospital and then pronounced dead, when he did not recover and failed to wake up. I do remember it caused trauma to the nurse as it would affect anyone who has to deal with this situation. This is when you have to have some level of emotional detachment in order to cope with traumatic situations. He had also written a suicide note addressed to his brother he was serving an IPP sentence with no release date and had already served many years and been in many prisons over the years. His brother was also a prisoner in a high security Cat A prison serving a sentence for murder and was housed in the psychiatric unit of that prison.

I did know this man because he had a CPAP machine, and I had seen him to review him and his machine and had ordered new parts for his machine. He was very polite and quiet and very grateful when I managed to get him the new hose and mask for his machine. He wasn't known really to healthcare because he didn't request any particular appointments or cause any issues and was not attending for any medication, so he was under the radar. They always say the quiet ones are always the worst. This man I can imagine that he had no hope of a life outside of prison and that his existence inside had got the better of him.

The worst thing is after a traumatic event like that, after you have documented all the details in the medical notes meticulously. It can take up to at least two years for the inquest. Which by then the event has become a memory and it is harder to remember with clarity the succession of events in the detail they may question you about. This caused a lot of stress and anxiety to the nurses and myself. Even though you know you did your utmost best at the time, you are questioned about it and feel that you are under the scrutiny of the judge.

If someone wants to carry out a hanging successfully, they will have planned it in advance and down to the last detail and will carry it out and have usually written and left a note. They will use bed sheets, they can plait them to make them stronger, clothing items, ripped up, or even the shower curtains. They were not issued with belts in the prison for this reason, but you would often see them wearing handmade belts, crafted from shreds of their bedsheets threaded through the belt loops of their prison issue jeans. Shoelaces were another item that could be used for strangulation, and the prison issue shoes and work boots and slippers had Velcro fastenings and were slip-on for this reason, although some wore their own trainers when allowed in the visits hall or during association time if they had the enhanced status and were deemed not to be at risk.

We had numerous calls to the wings when someone was threatening to hang themselves and there were many attempts usually when they didn't get their own way which happened frequently, and I described earlier as manipulative behaviour. It would more often be the younger prisoner who behaved like this. Before I worked there, I never knew that you could strangle yourself and cause asphyxiation without hanging off something but simply by lying on a bed or the floor. Some would tie the noose around their neck and around their ankles and feet with their legs bent and then straighten their legs and hold the pressure until it caused them to pass out. There was one young man who did this regularly at the same time as masturbating and gained sexual pleasure and gratification from this exercise. He was playing a dangerous game.

Some would stuff things into their mouths such as socks and then attempt asphyxiation on themselves to suffocate. I have heard of female prisoners using sanitary towels, swallowing them in pieces or using tissue paper which, when followed by drinking water would cause them to swell in the throat and cause choking. You must be pretty desperate and in a very dark place mentally to attempt this, but it happens, and people do die.

Swallowing items

We would get calls to the wings when prisoners had swallowed items. This quite often was batteries which we didn't have to send them in to hospital for when it was the normal AAA or AA type but when the lithium batteries started to be used in the vapes these were much more dangerous if swallowed. They can cause a hole to burn through the wall of the oesophagus, the stomach or the trachea which can be very dangerous and could be deadly. They would have to have an endoscopy, which is a camera inserted in order to allow the battery to be removed from the stomach.

The AA or AAA type of batteries rarely caused a problem. Beyond the oesophagus, they would usually be dissolved by the acid in the stomach and could be left to pass spontaneously as long as the patient remains asymptomatic. If they had become lodged in the oesophagus they should be removed within 2 hours. Because they could cause burns and life-threatening complications.

Usually, it was an attempt to get out of the prison and go to hospital and as discussed previously in the self-harm section, this could be due to boredom, and it was a distraction from the normality and daily grind of the prison regime. It could be just playing up because they had misbehaved and were unable to cope and knew they would be subjected to an adjudication for noncompliance of the rules, so they would retaliate to the disciplinary procedures and rules and escalate the situation with acts of self-harm and it was used as a way of coping.

One man also claimed to have swallowed the bleach tablets used for cleaning, although I don't know how he could possibly have managed to physically do this because it would have very quickly eroded his oesophagus. He would have been in an incredible amount of pain, but he had only reported vomiting symptoms and that was unwitnessed.

Another claimed to have swallowed pieces of a calculator, this led to lots of jokes such as, 'you couldn't add it up, and that was calculated, etc!!!

We could not prove whether they had swallowed items or not and we had to send them in to hospital which was incredibly frustrating because it took so much manpower and time to get them out and more often than not they would come back with negative toxicity blood levels when claiming to have swallowed items or taken an overdose but in fact they hadn't taken anything.

Overdoses

Other causes of death were the successful overdoses. One man had taken all of his antipsychotic medications and been found dead in the cell during the morning unlock. He was under the mental health team but was not currently active, meaning he was not on their caseload at the time and was only in his late thirties. This was an unexpected death, and he had not alerted anyone to feeling so low to the point of desperation. In this case there is little that can be done to stop them, because he had likely planned to do it and without any alerts or notifications to make anyone aware of his feelings how would anyone know of his intent?

There was another man who was well known to mental health and the nursing healthcare staff as he had been there many years and had had outbursts and difficult behaviour to manage at times, but over the later years of me being there he had calmed down and had a good job serving in the bistro. This was where the staff would go for lunch and have the food cooked and served by the prisoners. I don't know what caused him to take his overdose, but it could have been another knock back, having his parole refused for release, or progression to move to a lower category prison that caused him to do it. I never found out.

The nurses were called to his cell on the wing, right before they were due to go home because he had taken an overdose, and the officers were there at the cell door trying to calm him down and persuade him to have help.

He refused the nurses entry to his cell and would not let them go in to take his observations. They tried to explain to him that he would be very unwell and could die if he didn't go into hospital but the more, they tried to persuade him the angrier he became. He was shouting and swearing, very abusive and threatening to hurt them if they went near him, so they retracted and after documenting in the notes, there was little more they could do. After they had left to go home, he then became very drowsy and started to lose consciousness, so he was taken to hospital in a taxi by the officers and was semiconscious when they arrived at A and E. He was intubated and taken to the intensive care unit but died later on.

This is a difficult situation to handle because although they were trying their best to help him, they could not physically restrain him and force him to go, if the ambulance had turned up and he adamantly refused, they also would not have been able to forcefully take him in. This can only be done when they are sectioned under the mental health act and that takes time to get the documentation in order and processed by the correct people. They can also be taken in if they have lost consciousness and cannot refuse to go.

Luckily there were also a lot of people that were saved and a lot of cries for help, these were the unsuccessful attempts. A lot of which were due to behaviour from the younger ones who did not have good coping skills and had not learnt how to manage their emotions.

Cardiac Arrests

We also had several cardiac arrests during my time, some successful attempts at resuscitation saved them and others unfortunately were not. There was a younger prisoner who was a transgender and portraying as a woman. She was in her early forties and had a cardiac arrest, she was resuscitated successfully but when she returned to the prison, she put a complaint into the healthcare and was trying to sue us for resuscitating her!

The last one I was involved in happened in the morning, I was doing my clinic, and the code blue alarm was sounded and came over the radios. The other nurses were all busy and I was up in healthcare, so I grabbed the emergency bag and my colleague, a healthcare assistant, grabbed the oxygen and the defibrillator and we set off rapidly to the wing. The man, in his seventies was lying on his back with his head towards the door of the cell but half under the bed. He was not breathing and had no carotid pulse and was a deathly grey, we immediately put the defibrillator on him and started CPR, the first couple of chest compressions I did, I felt his ribs crack.

The code alarm meant an ambulance had been called by the comms team and was on its way. It was so cramped in the small cells I asked the officers to help me get him out into the corridor on the landing so we could work on him better. We inserted an I-gel into his airway to enable us to ventilate him with the ambubag and gave him oxygen through this. Several more nurses arrived and then the first responder from the ambulance service, so we soon got into a cycle, and kept rotating people with giving chest compressions so as to give good effective compressions without becoming tired.

The ambulance crew arrived and attached more equipment and started trying to place lines in him to give drugs intravenously, He was still showing no signs of life. The helicopter ambulance crew arrived next and undertook their assessment. We carried on with the CPR until they made the decision that it was not going to be successful and that we were not going to bring him back. He had several long-term conditions and had been on a lot of medications including those for his heart. It does give you a kick in the teeth when you can't do any more than you have tried to and are unsuccessful.

It leaves you feeling empty and even though I knew he was likely already dead when we reached him, it is disheartening when not successful and leaves you feeling low and flat. The other side is that you are so pumped on adrenaline when you arrive, and really from the second you respond to the alarm, because you don't know what you are going to be presented with fully until you arrive at the scene. You then perform as much as you can for as long as you need to until someone makes the decision to stop, or the patient starts to respond and recover. Once your adrenaline starts to reduce you feel deflated.

It was a very valuable experience especially for those nurses and healthcare assistants that had not previously worked on a patient before as it is different to performing CPR on the resus Annie that we use in our yearly mandatory training. The crews praised us in the effort we had applied and said we had worked really well as a team. we had performed the CPR for about fifty minutes in total.

About ten to fifteen minutes into the resuscitation another code blue alarm went and two of the nurses had to leave to go and attend a collapsed prisoner in the library, they also called the doctor to attend as there were no staff left in healthcare. When they arrived at the scene. there was a man on the floor crying out in pain, complaining of pain in his anus. He was rolling around on the floor and making a lot of noise and refusing to get up. One of the nurses suggested the doctor take a look because they were not getting anywhere with his diagnosis from questioning him. It turned out he had some thrombosing haemorrhoids, these are bulging piles, which were very painful. They did take him up to healthcare and the doctor actually lanced them to drain them and relieve the pressure, not something I would have been happy to perform but it seemed to quieten the man down. It saved him from having to go to hospital that day, but they took a good while, to settle and heal.

When something like this happens, we are invited to attend the debrief sessions the prison hold for their staff, which we went to, and it was worthwhile as we at least felt valued when they thanked us for our efforts. They offered us support if we wanted it to help cope psychologically.

The strangest part of that morning was the prison had a concert going on in the gardens of the grounds, they had prisoners playing instruments in a band in the grounds and some of them singing, for well-being day, The concert was not affected at all, whilst we were working in the midst of a crisis and although the ambulance crew and helicopter paramedics were arriving and nurses running around, they just carried on regardless and were completely unaware of what was happening. Some days it was a crazy place to work!

Falls

We had some very frail elderly men in the prison one had Parkinson's disease and very poor mobility. He had fallen out of his bed in the night and been lying on the floor for hours. He was unable to get up and when the officers arrived and began unlocking in the morning he was discovered. The nurses were called and after them assessing him an ambulance was called as they were also unable to get him up. The other concern was whether he had fractured his hip. It transpired that he developed a condition called rhabdomyolysis which is when injury to the muscle has occurred. The muscle cells are then damaged and break down leading to muscle death. When this happens, toxic components of the muscle fibres leak into the blood and kidneys and can cause kidney damage and life-threatening complications.

He must have been lying on the floor for many hours overnight and couldn't raise the alarm. He did go to hospital and did not recover and died.

Of course, this would have been investigated in great depth and there was a lot of questions asked that needed answering as to why he had been left so long without being discovered. The night officers check the prisoners through the door hatches and have this responsibility and have to raise the alarm if there are any concerns, that they feel warrant the opening of the cell or 'cracking the door' as it is known. They have to call the orderly officer and if they need to enter the cell, they have to get another officer and sometimes from another wing and the duty senior officer in charge as he has the overriding key and can give permission to open the cell door. As always it is a bit of a rigmarole when it is out of the normal working hours and structure of the day. It is breaking the 'night state' when there are minimal staff on duty and available to assist. It also creates extra paperwork which is also not best pleasing to have to complete.

The other case of rhabdomyolysis that also resulted in his death, I was directly involved in, and it affected me. I felt so bad for the poor man and felt it was definitely enhanced due to neglect, and I really can't believe that no one was punished for this. Well, maybe they were and quite rightly in my mind they should have been. Maybe I just didn't hear about it. I wouldn't be surprised if someone wasn't held accountable and sacked. The chances are that they were disciplined or reprimanded but the man had no supportive family or relatives to dispute the inquest and request answers to their questions of the results from the investigation into the cause of his death. The inquest was not one I was called to attend, or was involved in, so I never was aware of the outcome. There is always an inquest held into the cause of a death in custody, but it is not always disputed, and never if there is no one asking questions.

It involved a frail man who was in his seventies and had chronic obstructive pulmonary disease, COPD which is debilitating and is a chronic long term lung disease. He likely had other co-morbidities such as hypertension, (high blood pressure) and some degree of heart failure, but I cannot recall these in detail. He definitely had poor mobility, some of this was caused by arthritis but mostly it was caused from years of struggling to breathe and reduced lung function following many years of smoking and damage to his lungs.

He had just returned from a stay in hospital and had been diagnosed with Covid, and a chest infection, so his lung capacity was even further reduced, and he was feeling very weak, and his mobility had deteriorated even more. At that time the hospitals were full to capacity, and they were discharging patients early when they weren't always ready and were still requiring care and support. They do not always understand how the prison healthcare works and think that because there is a healthcare department, that we are able to provide more care than we actually can. We did not have a 24-hour care provision in place and the prisoners have to be self-caring and are locked up from 19.00 hours for around 12 hours overnight.

During the Covid pandemic this was even longer and for those that we knew were Covid positive they were locked up until they had had two negative Covid test results on two consecutive days. This could result in many days in isolation. So, he was literally locked up in his cell and checked on by the officers unlocking the door in the morning and getting him to swab himself and hand back the swab test each morning. He would have been given his meals and that would have been the only contact with others he would have received. When he arrived back from the hospital the wing officers had notified healthcare that he was back so that he could have been checked by healthcare by a nurse. This wasn't always very forthcoming information that we received in a timely manner and if they returned after the nurses had gone home this could be many hours later and not until the next day.

It was documented in his notes that he had been checked by the nurse, but due to the state of him being Covid positive he had only been seen from the door and he had answered that he felt ok. He had his medications in his possession in his cell and understood how to take them. All physical contact was being kept to the minimum needed, to reduce the risk of contamination and spread of Covid. I cannot recall that he had had his observations of oxygen saturation level, blood pressure, heart rate, respiratory rate and temperature recorded in his notes following his return from hospital, but he had at least been physically seen.

We received the call to attend the wing as soon as we had arrived to start the shift at the beginning of the day when the officers had unlocked the cells. They could not see him through the hatch, so instead of just turning the key to unlock the cell, they had to physically push open the door to look in and they could see him sitting on the toilet, he was barely responding to their attention, and he couldn't get up. They put out a code blue and myself and my nursing colleague attended. We put on the PPE personal protective equipment which was carried in another pack which had been added to the emergency bag, alongside the oxygen and the defibrillator. We arrived at the officers gathered around the outside of his cell, none of whom had entered the cell and were unwilling to enter, none had put on their PPE and were clearly waiting for us.

The poor man was frozen cold, he had been sitting on that toilet, it transpired since the evening before and had sat there all night. He was peripherally shut down and was purple in colour, we couldn't get an oxygen saturation level from the pulse oximeter due to his circulation having been drawn from the extremities i.e. his fingers and toes, back into his internal organs to protect them and supply the oxygen to his heart and lungs. We had an ambulance en route. I had a lot of difficulty getting a blood pressure reading from him, due to it being in his boots. In other words, this was very low, again the body's mechanism is to protect the heart. He had a pulse, but this was slow and difficult to feel. I had to take it from his carotid artery in his neck as I was unable to palpate the wrist pulse. He was barely conscious, and he was also very deaf, so he had great difficulty in hearing us.

We attempted to get him to stand, to get him off the toilet but he had no strength in his leg muscles to push himself up, or his arm muscles to hold his grab rail to pull himself up. I asked the officers for blankets and to get him a hot drink which they did with sugar in it to try and get him to warm up. We were also finding it very difficult to try and assist him with standing due to the extremely small space we were working in with him on the toilet and the cells are small enough spaces with one person in. Add to those two nurses, the bags and equipment and officers in the doorway, it was a very cramped space. We tried to keep as much equipment out of the cell at the time to a minimum and restricted what we needed to use as necessary to be brought into the cell. We also had him on oxygen.

The ambulance arrived after some time and of course they had to don their full PPE. They had some straps and with their assistance we were able to assist in getting him up. He had a deep indentation on the back of his thighs and buttocks from having sat on there for more than 12 hours. The ambulance crew were shocked that he had been left that long and they actually filed a safeguarding concern to the local health authority to have this incident investigated.

The wing observation record sheet I saw, had hourly observations recorded by the same officer on the night duty. The entries had been made hourly throughout the night and were in the same handwriting for the whole shift. It read, 'on the toilet, no response'.

There were initial entries from the evening shift stating he was observed on the toilet from around 1700hrs and that he was not responding when asked if he was ok. We had been called to the wing around 07.30 am, that was already fourteen hours later.

It was diabolical and as he was profoundly deaf, he would not have heard them if they had asked if he was ok. He also would not have actually been visible from looking through the door hatch. They would have physically had to crack the door, open it, and look in to see that he was actually still on the toilet. All they would have been able to ascertain is that he was not on his bed or chair or visible through the hatch! No one, even if they had a bad case of diarrhoea would stay on the toilet that long without getting up.

If he had been able to hear them, he would have known there was someone there and been able to shout for help. I still find it difficult to believe that someone would leave another person who was frail and elderly all night long on the toilet and not check them thoroughly enough to get a response. They are employed to provide care to those in custody. The entries did not change line after line, just the time on the left column of when the check was made. It looked to me to have been completed all in one go, and in retrospect of the event, when you are catching up on your paperwork early in the morning and at the end of your shift. Call me suspicious, but I would say the checks hadn't been made. Yes, this is accusatory but that's what I think happened. It resulted in that man's death.

Healthcare Team

We were awesome and we did win 'Team of the Year' one year within our NHS Trust, it was well deserved and really made us appreciate how strong we were as a team. We enjoyed going out for an evening to have a meal and party together and were honoured to receive the award.

Our prison healthcare team were quite unique in that most of the nursing staff once permanently employed, seemed to stay for a long time and many, up until their retirement. There was such diversity in the day to day events in nursing, I thought it would be very hard to get bored in this role because things were always happening and there were always new changes to adapt to, both within the prison and the nursing and healthcare side of things. Other prisons ran mainly on agency nursing staff who did not settle into permanent roles and this is hard to work with when people don't work continually within the team, the patients do not benefit from any continuity of care and just working from one shift to another, some things would get missed in future planning, simply just not booking the next appointment for a wound dressing or not ordering the next injection for example could cause wasted time and appointments. It was frustrating for both us and the patients. Especially those who needed pushing over in a wheelchair by one of the other prisoners and then needed to use the stair lift to come upstairs to healthcare to then discover there hadn't been an appointment booked for him in a clinic for his dressing or he had no injection ordered and would have to wait two days until it was prescribed, reordered and then until it arrived!

Other prisons did not retain staff well and this was more than likely due to the burn out or violence or repeatedly struggling to work with staff shortages which meant the nurses that were left on duty had to work twice as hard to enable the day-to-day work was completed.

One of the main duties of prison nursing especially in the higher category prisons which had a higher level of security and had much riskier prisoners, was the administration of medication. This was an endless cycle of medication rounds due to them not being able to have their medications in possession. The risks were of overdose to themselves and of trading with others. We had an added risk of failure to comply with some of the more elderly or confused patients remembering to take their medications correctly, especially if they were diabetic and required insulin which would be dangerous if they did not remember to take it correctly, and could end up with them having to go out to hospital, if they became very unwell.

I remember when I was contemplating applying for and accepting the job as a prison nurse I contacted a colleague who I knew had left the hospital wards and gone into prison nursing to ask her views and she told me you need to be careful not to get deskilled because a lot of the daily nursing activities is medications. It couldn't have been more wrong in my case.

Shortly after starting I undertook a minor illness course so I could deal with most of the day-to-day complaints that we encountered in the clinics. I had previously nursed on a respiratory support and sleep centre for the past 13 years which was quite a speciality in a hospital, very different from prison nursing. I think one of the hardest parts of the job initially was not so much as making a decision to send a patient out to hospital if you had assessed them and were not comfortable to leave them in the prison, at weekends or evenings on the late shift you had to work autonomously without any backup from the doctors, because there were no doctors on duty out of hours. We had access to calling the out of hour's community doctor's service on the phone, but they would not know the patients, like we did, nor did they understand how the prison regime or protocols worked.

It was the battle that sometimes ensued between yourself and the prison governors, orderly officers or the custodial managers, as they were now called, who could make you feel very guilty. They would say, 'you're joking? No Miss, we haven't got enough staff to send him out, it's Sunday afternoon!' I would feel very guilty, and it initially put me off, but I learnt to become more confident and actually, that was not my problem.

If I had decided that someone needed to go out to hospital then, they needed to go, it was better to be safe than sorry. This happened once within my first 2 years of working there, my radio went off announcing a code red and calling the nurse to the astro turf where I found the patient sprawled out in a star shape on his back in pain where he had twisted his knee and gone down playing football. The physical education instructors, PEIs had witnessed it and called me over, I applied ice to his knee we managed to get him up and into a wheelchair and I gave him both paracetamol and ibuprofen, he said he had felt something snap, so although he was obviously in some pain, his observations were stable and he then managed to sing me some songs whilst we took him back to his wing. I was discussing sending him out to hospital for an x-ray but was informed it would be near enough impossible for them to supply any officers to manage the escort.

I was under pressure and we were also employed by the prison service at the time so I telephoned the local accident and emergency department at the hospital and discussed the patient with them who advised the usual advice of RICE – Rest, Ice, Elevation, Compression and said that even if he were to come in they only had radiographers on call on the weekends so he would probably stay in A & E or stay on a ward overnight and be x-rayed in the morning. I ensured he had enough painkillers to take for the rest of the day and overnight, I bandaged his knee and had an ice pack on his knee and made sure he had a jug to enable him to use if he needed to urinate in case he couldn't get to the toilet and left a message for the doctor to ensure he was reviewed first thing in the morning. He could also call the officers if his pain became unbearable, and they could have sent him in to hospital in the night if needed. Anyway, the long and short of it was that yes, he was sent into hospital the next morning and he had sustained a fracture which he had surgery on, and a pin and plate inserted to repair and strengthen it.

I had essentially done nothing wrong in my management of him and had sought advice but had still felt guilty for not being more assertive and insisting on sending him in there and then. The outcome would not have changed for him, but he decided to sue for compensation which unfortunately is a common occurrence and past time it seems for some prisoners, remember they have a lot of time on their hands. Also, since then, the Healthcare department in the prison was taken over by a National Health Service (NHS) trust. This I think has made us even more autonomous in our decision-making skills.

As far as the litigation went, he initially lost his case, but he disputed the decision and as long as seven years later he eventually got a compensation pay out for, he claims,' being left in agony and not sent straight into hospital'. So, this has made me more wary, but I still only send those I firmly believe need to go out and it hasn't made me so overcautious as to send everyone.

I then progressed in my career by being asked if I would take on the substance misuse case load as a nurse manager because the clinical lead had handed in her notice with the enticement of pastures new. I initially was not keen, thinking, I don't know anything about it and had never had to deal with these types of patients before, at least before I had worked in the prison.

When I initially started in the prison, during the first days of giving out the medication, I was shocked to have to ask them to open their mouths to show me they had swallowed their medication and not pushed it into their cheek or hidden it under their tongue. This was a totally new concept and not something you normally came across or thought about in nursing. In prisons some of the medication is highly tradable and can be used to barter and a lot of bullying happens because of this.

Although the prisoners don't handle cash or physical money, they have accounts which money can be paid into from their families or friends and associates, and a lot of deals can be made through these sources especially if they manage to get access to a mobile phone to arrange payments. This is also true of trafficking of drugs or phones through visitors or corrupt staff that may act as mules and bring illicit items into the establishment. There is a lot of corruption within prisons and pressure is often put onto the vulnerable to perform illicit acts.

In order to be employed in a prison a very detailed vetting security check has to be undertaken to check you are not in debt or owe considerable amounts of money or have substantial loans to pay off, which increases your susceptibility to being vulnerable to accept bribes. This can also be pressure applied by other prisoners to the weak and the elderly who can be bullied easily for their medication or forced to ask the doctor for strong pain relief for arthritis for the elderly, or sleeping tablets. During the time I have worked there we have become very robust in medicines management and pain management and have a strong multi-disciplinary team working ethic which makes it strong and united.

The management and decision making is made easier all round when we are unanimous in our approach. We had no qualms when it came to stopping medication for someone who has been caught attempting to conceal their medication and divert it. If they are not taking it themselves and are trading it, then they don't need it, and it is unsafe to continue to prescribe it.

The message soon gets around and deters others who have been doing the same. We rarely get much feedback once they have stopped because they know they are wrong. Those that do try to pursue it usually hit a brick wall because their solicitors will write in and demand to know when we are going to restart their clients medication and how dare we stop it when they are in agonising pain, the client has usually forgotten to tell them that actually they were caught attempting to divert their medication and that they are actually employed and working or have been witnessed to be climbing up and down the ladders of a bunk bed where they sleep on the top, or that they go to the gym 3 times a week and have been witnessed to be bench pressing 80kg weights doing 3 sets of 25 repetitions 3 times a week.

Others have been caught on CCTV cameras using their crutch or walking stick as a weapon to hit another prisoner and one actually jumped out of his electric wheelchair to throw a punch at another, so their pain sometimes miraculously disappears. It reminded me of the scene on 'Little Britain' on TV, where he jumps out of the wheelchair, runs around and is fully mobile then gets back into his wheelchair before his friend who pushes the wheelchair has time to see him.

Our patient was diabetic and when he didn't get his own way with something, he would stop taking his medications. It would then make him become quite ill and many times he was sent out to hospital as he required stabilising before it was safe for him to come back.

It was always self-inflicted and created a dilemma for us nurses because he definitely needed to take his diabetes medication regularly and monitor his blood glucose levels, but he refused to do so during these times. We were busy enough and the officers would ring to ask us to deliver his medication to his cell, but we also had both sides of the prison to administer medications to. We felt we were playing into his hands, and he was displaying manipulative behaviour and getting away with it, and he knew it.

They shout and swear and sometimes become violent or start self-harming to manipulate the situation and the officers would sometimes ring to ask when they can have their medication back. The prisoners would threaten us with their solicitors, saying they would sue us. I would calmly explain that their solicitors are not prescribers and do not have the qualification to restart their medications; neither do they have keys or the authority to come into the prison, which generally quietens them down!

I had a patient who was on my substance misuse caseload and was serving an IPP sentence, with no release date. He arrived on a methadone prescription and was in his fifties. He was on a very low dose of 10mls of methadone and he had been on this dose for the last few years. It was barely above a therapeutic dose. He was also on a prescription of Pregabalin which I have covered before and not safe to continue to prescribe both. He was well known for manipulative behaviour in his last prison and every couple of years seemed to end up in the segregation unit and end up being transferred to another prison, but he did not want to give up his methadone. I heard he had climbed onto the roof at his last prison in a protest.

We held the routine 13:week review consultation meeting and we discussed the safety around the co-prescribed medications and advised we would have to start thinking about which medication he would consider coming off, he asked if he could switch over from methadone to subutex, which people say is a nicer medication to reduce down from and gives less side effects. As I mentioned before it was also highly tradeable and sought after and for this reason, we only switched people over onto it if they wanted to detox and come off their prescription of opiate substitute medication completely or if they were being released into the community.

When they were given an actual release, date and we were able to have this confirmed in writing, we could switch them onto subutex and titrate them up to an agreed dose to ensure they remained stable when released into the community and this way they were less likely to start using illicit drugs again. They would also have to engage regularly with the community substance misuse services, and this should reduce their chance of reoffending.

I clearly explained to him that we would only agree to this if he was sure he wanted to start a reduction and detox off his very low dose of methadone. If it turned out he changed his mind and didn't want to complete the detox, he could go back onto methadone, but we would then have to start reducing the Pregabalin, but we would not keep prescribing both of these. He agreed , we wrote the plan out which was to go without methadone the next day completely and the day after he would be started on subutex at a low dose (the equivalent of the 10mls of methadone), then every 3 days he would reduce the dose until he finished the course.

Methadone is a long-acting drug and was only given once every 24 hours because it stays in the system and has a long half-life. If we gave the subutex too soon, before the methadone effects had completely cleared then it could bring on precipitated withdrawal symptoms which would not be nice to deal with, hence the reason for omitting the next day's methadone dose. The subutex was much shorter acting and lasted approximately 6 hours before starting to be cleared. People who have had methadone for years complain of aches in their bones.

We all signed the plan, and his substance misuse case worker was in attendance and was aware that he would need additional support to help him through the next few weeks. As he was on such a low dose of methadone he would be off the medications in just over 2 weeks. So, we started the process and then he started with his behaviour. Literally after taking his first dose of subutex, he started asking for the dose to be increased, we advised him, he would be sticking to the plan. He was demanding to see me for an appointment to discuss this and refused to leave healthcare unless I saw him immediately. I said I would see him later that morning if there was an appointment slot available. He would not go back to the wing but remained in the waiting room.

After tea we had finished the medications, I telephoned his key worker and asked her to also attend as I felt I may need a witness to the consultation. He sat I. The chair and became louder and louder shouting and demanding I prescribe him a higher dose of subutex,

I remained calm and advised him this was not going to happen and that he needed to calm down, the case worker was looking concerned and she got up to exit the room at the point of me standing and opening the door for her to leave and me asking him to leave the room. He refused to move and clung onto the chair, the officer outside the room had heard all the noise along with my colleagues down the corridor and they were beginning to start getting concerned for my safety and move towards my room to check if I was ok. As he was clearly not calming down and gripping the arms of the chair, I left the room and stepped into the corridor, he then jumped up and ran into the corridor and the waiting room, my colleague had pressed the general alarm button in healthcare and raised the alarm bell. The officer on duty in healthcare stepped towards him to try and talk to him and at that point, he threw himself onto the floor like a toddler and was flailing both arms and legs and was lying flat on his back in the middle of the waiting room floor, screaming, 'arrest me, arrest me, ' at the top of his lungs ! He reminded me of an upturned tortoise. There were other prisoners sitting in the waiting room, but as another 6-8 officers arrived promptly, on the scene, they soon cleared the others out. The guy was now holding both his hands above his head ready to be handcuffed. No one had laid a finger on him, but he was acting as though he had been rugby tackled to the floor. It was very comical to watch, very over exaggerated and a good bit of acting, anyway as he wouldn't calm down or stop shouting, the officers just picked him up and carried him still shouting off down to the seg.

Of course, one of the duty governors rang me up and asked if I could increase his subutex dose as he had asked for it. I calmly went down to discuss and explain what the situation was and that I believed he had been trying to get onto the subutex and then have it increased with no intention at all of reducing and he thought he was going to stay on that prescription as well. He was used to using manipulation to achieve what he wanted, but little did he know that we were robust and stuck to the plan we had agreed upon.

He was in the segregation unit then and having to be escorted up to the healthcare to receive his medication with two officers every morning. He was self-harming and cutting himself, still in an attempt to get what he wanted. He smeared blood all over the walls of the stairwell all the way through healthcare just to create work for someone who would then have to clean it up. It actually made it easier whilst he was in the seg because there was much less chance of him obtaining any other illicit drugs or medication whilst down there, if he thought he may up the ante and perhaps take an overdose. So, whilst down there we continued the reduction plan, and he finished the prescription of his substance misuse medication, and he was returned to the wing.

Several days later, just before lunchtime, we had a call from the wing saying that he had fallen down the stairs on the wing. The duty doctor attended with one of the nurses as the wing officers said he was screaming in agony, and they couldn't get him up and were scared to move him as he was making so much noise.

It was an unwitnessed fall and considering it was a busy time of day at association time when all the prisoners were unlocked and getting ready to collect their lunches from the hatches on the wings, there were many other people around and officers, but no one saw it happen.

When the doctor arrived at the scene, he was lying upside down on the stairs in other words his head end was lower than his legs. When he saw the doctor, he started getting louder and louder and demanding to go to hospital. He was claiming to have broken his back. The doctor had worked in many prisons and was not one to be fooled. He told the prisoner to stop fooling around and get up. He then went straight to the office to document this in the prison wing observation book and left the wing and returned to healthcare. The prisoner and probably the officers couldn't quite believe it, but it made him get up and he then walked back to his cell normally.

He manipulated the wing staff into getting hold of a wheelchair for him due to his alleged fall, even though he had not been observed and the doctor had not believed him. The officers got him a wheelchair and he was seen doing wheelies in it on the wing landing. This resulted in him going over backwards in the wheelchair and he fell out of it. As he had not got what he wanted from the nursing team in healthcare, he then demanded that he be seen by mental health.

There was another prisoner who claimed to need a wheelchair for an injured back, he spent over 18 months attending healthcare twice a day in his wheelchair to collect his medication. This was morphine and was a controlled drug. He had another prisoner who was his wheelchair pusher to bring him over to healthcare in the wheelchair and they spent over half an hour each time, sometimes longer, sitting at the bottom of the stairwell waiting for the nurses to bring down his medication which he then took under supervision with a mouth check.

He had a full assessment undertaken for the provision of a new wheelchair which involved someone coming into the prison to do the assessment from social services. All the time he was receiving disability benefits which he was entitled to, and which was paid into his bank account.

One day we caught him diverting his morphine tablet, which he had dropped into his lap, obviously his mouth was clear but that was him caught. From that day on he was commenced on a reduction plan of his medication. It took several months to wean him down from the morphine until he was off it. He then was seen easily and freely walking around the wing, with no wheelchair, and had it seemed made a miraculous recovery!

Of course, now he had been caught out he no longer had to pretend to be disabled, his benefits were stopped and there was no point him carrying on with this charade.

So, after my agreeing to the 6-month secondment of managing the substance misuse caseload of patients, I actually found I enjoyed it and appeared to do it well. This then led on to me undertaking my Non-Medical Prescribing course. This was a 6-month course and was the hardest intense course I had ever undertaken. My boss at the time, was right when he told me to put my life on hold for the 6 months, and don't commit to anything else but getting through the course. He was so right, it consumes you day and night and is stressful, but it was also the best course to have done and to have achieved the qualification as it increases your autonomy twofold.

No more waiting for prescriptions to be written. We were lucky that our pharmacist and pharmacy department were so efficient in getting medications and urgently when required and we had a wide selection of drugs available to use under a Patient Group Direction (PGD) which was so useful during out of hours, evenings and weekends. Having the qualification to prescribe meant that the nurses could also request prescriptions from me as well as the doctor and the pharmacist who also took the course after me.

I was able to write all the prescriptions for the Methadone and opiate substitute treatments which was really useful if we happened to have receptions coming in late in the afternoon or doctors who were not familiar with substance misuse and were reluctant to write prescriptions for.

Security

The security department were good at communication of intelligence reports which were sent to me by email. The problem was you never knew who had submitted them and therefore their reliability was not guaranteed. There were numerous reports about prescribed medication – suspicion of people trading their medication and names were mentioned. This would then instigate a medication compliance check which would be carried out by either the nurses or the pharmacy technician and involved going to their cells with an officer and asking to see their medication which would then be counted in front of them and should tally with the amount they should have had. This had to be calculated from their last collection and the amount they were allowed in possession.

We had a medication compact which they were all asked to sign upon arrival at the prison which clearly stated that they must take their medication correctly and as prescribed. They would not remove tablets from the named packaging or store it in separate containers, it also clearly said that if there was any suspicion of attempting to conceal their medication or divert it for trading then the prescription would be reviewed and a decision would be made and the medication was more often than not, be discontinued either slowly as a reducing dose or stopped immediately, depending on the circumstances.

The intelligence received covered all aspects in the prison including bullying, violence, sexual acts, relationships and other illicit items; they also covered mental health and reported when prisoners had begun to act bizarrely and exhibiting concerning behaviours. It was a good system to ensure the allegations were looked into by the correct department.

There was also a monthly global newsletter sent to all departments from Security which notified of any illicit items found around the prison and from cell searches, weapons which had been made, one of the latest being a large cross bow which I mentioned earlier. It was made entirely from matchsticks and was extremely strong as it had been bound by a heavy-duty glue. It also had sharpened pencils which were very effective arrows and would have caused injury. He had also written an instruction manual on how to make one with diagrams included. When he was sent for the adjudication for making it, he innocently claimed, it was his first time in prison and that he wasn't aware that this was not allowed! He also said he had made it as a present to give his son!

A lot of the prisoners made some very impressive models to pass the time with intricate detail. These included picture frames, trinket boxes, clock surrounds, a windmill, a birdcage, gypsy wagons and horses, made from matchsticks. These were allowed as a hobby and crafting. Others did needlecraft and cross stitching. One man did a large tapestry picture of another prison building in London which was amazing the amount of work that had gone into it.

There were a lot of impressive artists who did sketches and paintings, which can be seen around the prison on walls and in some of the corridors and on the landings, there were some beautiful murals which certainly brightened up the place. We had another man who folded thousands of pieces of individual card in different colours and made models of animals, lots of birds, owls, parrots and mice- which he gave out and some of them could be used as pen holders.

Another had suffered with cancer and received chemotherapy and radiotherapy and he used his talents to create cards which we displayed up in healthcare and sold for any donations which he always gave to the Macmillan charity for nurses to show how grateful he was for the care he received when going out to have chemotherapy and radiotherapy at the hospital.

Employment

All of the prisoners had to be assigned some activities to do during the day these included employment, education and the gym. Some of the older prisoners of retirement age didn't have to work but were encouraged to participate in activities to prevent them getting bored some were voluntary activities such as being a wheelchair pusher a listener or a representative for other prisoners, these could be for LGBGT , racial equality, traveller groups, transgender, gym orderlies, mental health trainers, healthcare trainers, and substance misuse reps, some of these were paid and some not. The listeners were used in a way similar to the Samaritans and were made available to visit other prisoners. They were invaluable, especially for prisoners struggling to cope with their sentences or for those serving sentences for the first time and those feeling suicidal and depressed. This could also include those that had just been knocked back from a parole hearing when they genuinely thought they would be released, and the decision had been a refusal of a release.

Education was provided for those having left school with little or no qualifications and they could gain basic maths, English, language, computer technology, art and creativity in writing courses and qualifications. For those wanting to gain skills in trades, there were bricklaying, carpentry, painting and decorating, and car mechanics courses they could undertake and also gain qualifications.

There were workshops where they went to do paid employment, some of the work included installing speaking panels into microwaves for blind people to use, making key rings, and camouflage nets to name a few. They also used to fill the little plastic eggs with the toys that are sold inside the kinder chocolate eggs, but someone got hold of this information and provided it to a local newspaper which caused quite a stir as the public deemed it to not be appropriate or suitable for the prisoners associated with sex crimes to be undertaking such work. As kinder eggs are made primarily for children and there were many prisoners who were registered on the sex offenders register.

COVID 19

I cannot exclude this from the book as it was something which has never before happened in my lifetime and was so unpredictable and came from out of the blue and continued for so long impacting not only on our work inside the prison but was a worldwide pandemic and drained on the resources of the NHS across all nations and countries. Of course, every year before Covid 19 we gave the yearly flu vaccinations when they arrived in and for several weeks of the year, healthcare concentrated most of the clinics around vaccinating the patients who were eligible to receive it.

The outbreaks of infectious diseases we were used to dealing with every year was the Norovirus (causing sickness and diarrhoea) which when it hit did tend to spread through the wings fairly quickly. We were used to reporting daily figure to the Department of Health and the Health

Protection Agency informing them if we had any outbreaks of infectious diseases. These included Hepatitis B and C, Tuberculosis, Flu, Measles, Mumps, and Legionnaires disease, to name a few on the list.

When the Covid-19 pandemic started it was difficult to believe, that it was going to affect us as you feel like you are within the walls of the prison and a small establishment compared to out in the community. No one really knew how quickly it was going to spread or how devastating it was going to be. We were invaded by information which was sent in thick and fast and before you had a chance to read the first piece of information you were being bombarded with more from all different governing bodies, the Department of Health, the Health Protection Agency, the Care and Quality Commission, the Trust, Public Health England, the National Institute of Clinical Excellence (NICE) and the trust's infection control department. No one really understood how it had started and how serious it was to become and affect the numbers of people it has, sadly resulting in millions of deaths.

There were many conspiracy theories being branded around and quickly from the onset we were told to wear protective personal equipment (PPE) masks and to maintain a 2-metre distance for others. This is very difficult when caring for patients and undertaking dressings or taking observations. Initially it appeared Healthcare were the only ones wearing the face masks, gloves and aprons and prison staff were getting anxious that they weren't being provided with the same level of protection and they also work in close contact with the prisoners. A while later they were advised to wear the face masks and then a lot of the officers began to complain as they did not want to wear them, you can never keep everyone happy. It was the same with the prisoners.

As they began to isolate patients, those classed as vulnerable (meaning they had a diagnosis of an existing health condition), began to receive letters sent by the government advising them to shield, the healthcare workload increased rapidly. Most of the prisoners were locked up behind their doors for increasing amounts of time. Initially we had to bottle up the entire see to take medications including the methadone and other controlled drugs and transport them around the prison and deliver them cell to cell. It was very time consuming and increased the risks of errors happening but thankfully very few were made. Many officers went off and were shielding from work if they had any underlying health conditions, along with some from healthcare. Most of the non- uniformed staff i.e. teachers, workers from education and programmes went onto furlough due to the industries, workshops education and the gym being shut down so no daily activities were running. The PE instructors were usually assigned to healthcare to escort us around the prison to deliver the medications which we were more than happy with, and it meant we were getting our steps in for the day and it did help us to develop good communication with the officers who helped us out considerably and saved a lot of time by opening the cell doors for us.

The pharmacy staff did an incredible job for months. They had to deliver the medications, endlessly, all the in possession, monthly, weekly and some of the daily medications to the individual cells. They also went out to the cells for the medication rounds, alongside the nurses, to administer the seem to take medications to those prisoners who had supervised consumption meds around the whole establishment. This they achieved with a very small number of staff. We all worked incredibly hard, day in and day out for the ensuing months. Everybody pulled together and most of the healthcare department suffered with COVID which also increased the workload for a time as we all worked so closely together, and it was inevitable that this would happen. Luckily, we were all fine and recovered fully with no long-term effects, but I know there have been thousands who have lost colleagues and family and friends, and it has been a truly shocking experience. Nobody had ever experienced anything like the Covid 19 pandemic before. The worldwide pandemic that no one could have predicted how long it lasted for and how things were going to run. We coped with the new challenges as they occurred and came up with solutions, time and time again.

We did have outbreaks across the prison and luckily each time managed extremely well to contain the spread every time a case was discovered by locking down spurs, landings and wings at a time to contain it. We also had some patients who died during Covid, and these deaths have been classed as Covid related deaths, but they all had underlying health conditions. They had been sent into hospital unwell and whilst in hospital, their swabs showed with positive results. This indicates they must have contracted it from the hospital as it was on the wards. We had others who went out unwell with Covid symptoms and recovered and returned.

We had to undertake swabbing, of any suspected cases, as they arrived as transfers in, and they had to be isolated behind their doors for 14 days and have 2 negative test result swabs before being allowed to circulate on the wing. They let people out in bubbles but as soon as they were let off the wings when the workshops opened or to go to exercise at the gym they would merge with other bubbles.

We also had to test swab patients who had upcoming hospital appointments prior to going to hospital to ensure they were negative before attending their appointment. The introduction of telephone and video consultations started which we will continue to use as it is saving a lot of money by not having to use two escorting officers to each hospital appointment.

The virus also swept through the officers who again brought it back into the prison because if they were handcuffed to escort a prisoner out to hospital and had been in contact with someone outside who had had the virus, then it was passed on. Of course, some people had the virus but were asymptomatic so unless they were swabbed, they would have been undetected and not known. The officers also have to work in close proximity of each other and of the prisoners, especially when they are involved in a control or restraint procedure and in reality, there is never enough time to stand there and glove and gown up in an emergency situation.

The other issue was how we would get to know when patients needed to be seen, obviously ill patients were detected by the prison wing staff and notified to healthcare, but as there was no free movement, we no longer were running the triage system that had run before where patients could come up and book appointments for various members of the healthcare team. We set up the application form system so they could fill in a form and request an appointment to be seen. There were health trainers or other prisoners on the wings who could help if they had difficulty communicating or with literacy.

I had started another course, Advanced Assessment and Clinical Reasoning skills and this required me to gain a minimum of 40 cases which were physical examinations of the different systems of the body and required to be assessed by a doctor.

Initially I was working through this in the clinical treatment rooms but once the prison started in lock down and there were no movements, there was no way we could allow patients up into the Healthcare department. So off I went with the doctors on their rounds across the establishment, cell to cell to undertake the examinations. We took the personal protective equipment (PPE) in the doctor's bag and just got on with it as you have to be adaptable in every situation.

Some of the interactions in the cells were difficult as they are very cramped and if they were sharing cells, we had to ask the cell mate to wait outside in the corridor to maintain confidentiality. We also required a prison officer to escort us around as we do not carry cell door keys, but this is a security issue and made it safer for us. We made do, the best we could with the situation. The most frustrating incidences were when we called ambulances or were trying to send patients into hospital for investigations and because they were unwell. The hospitals really didn't want to admit extras because they were filling up with Covid cases and after a struggle for us getting them transferred in, they then sent them back too early it seemed, because they still were unwell. We had to send them back in again, if they were too unwell to stay in the prison, because they are left unsupervised for long periods in their cells with no one to watch them.

Anyway, we got there, and I got a lot of experiences, developed a good rapport with the doctors and the newer doctors appreciated me escorting them around as they were new to working in the prison environment and were unfamiliar with the way things work here. They quickly learnt their way around the wings. They also had to adapt greatly as they usually worked as General Practitioners (GPs) in the community setting, in surgeries and undertook the occasional house visits. This was indeed an eye opener for some. I am pleased to say I did pass my course and gained the qualification as an Advanced Nurse Practitioner of which I am very proud.

After the first wave of the pandemic, we relaxed the rules slightly and those who were in receipt of controlled drugs had to attend Healthcare twice a day to take their medication, but were collected from their wings by the officers, and escorted over which was much more time consuming. They were collected wing by wing and then returned before the next wing could be collected and brought over.

This went on for months throughout the summer and then as we started relaxing the restrictions as per the governments instructions, the second wave hit and we were back in lockdown, with children being home schooled. Some of the nurses were having difficulty getting their children into school as they had to book them in through a booking system and although the parents were key workers, they didn't always automatically get given a place, so childcare became an issue. It was wearing and took its toll. Holidays had been cancelled throughout the year and no one was allowed to go anywhere so it was a hard time, but we were a strong team, and we ploughed on through.

During the second wave, the prison started lateral flow testing for all staff working in the prison establishment, for all departments for both directly and non-directly employed staff. These were conducted twice weekly, and they would notify anyone whose test showed positive the same day. The number of cases within the prison started to rise due to it being brought in by staff as it did in the community, staff went off sick to isolate and an outside company came in and swab tested all of the prisoners. This was a big operation which took a few days to complete and resulted in several spurs and some wings to be locked down to contain it. This did work and within a few weeks things settled, and no new cases emerged. We then came off the red list as being an outbreak site and were able to plan ahead.

After the second wave we began to think about restoration. We began to run clinics on the healthcare sites with limited numbers of patients allowed in the waiting rooms and 2 metre distancing rules, face masks to be worn and some of the outside contracted services began to run again, the dentist, optician, podiatrist, ultra-sonographer, physiotherapist started to return. The problem was the waiting lists had become tremendous and there was a backlog of patients across all of the waiting lists.

To add to the workload we already had, as routine clinics had not been run for a long period of time all of the patients with chronic conditions normally monitored 6 monthly or even yearly had missed their reviews. These clinics were started up which left no free hands-on deck. The next programme we had to undertake was the Covid vaccinations. This was an incredible task which myself and my colleague took on with two others doing the administration of documentation and entering into the patients records. We worked our way through over 900 patients who received their first vaccinations and at the time of writing this, section of my book, we had given almost 700 of their second vaccinations. We then received notification that we would be giving a third dose as a booster alongside the yearly flu vaccinations. An incredible task, but we deserved a big pat on the back, even though I say it myself, for us, the administrators and of course pharmacy that had to plan and receive the ordering, and storage of the vaccines.

Litigation

This is a subject which is definitely on the rise across the UK, and definitely within the NHS, medical and nursing sectors and is increasing every year. It used to be the USA that you heard about suing people and businesses, but it has become more commonplace especially in the last three decades and it continues to rise.

I mentioned a patient suing healthcare for not being sent out to hospital immediately for a fractured leg which he had pinned and plated. He still received the same treatment and likely would have still had to wait until the next day for his surgery as he was stable when he was admitted to hospital and would have to have waited for a theatre slot.

He attempted to sue three times, and it was rejected twice but he was persistent and on the third attempt he received compensation 7 years later, despite his leg having been repaired.

Some of the prisoners spent their time on building their cases against the prison and also healthcare in order to gain some monetary compensation, and if they were dismissed, they would then appeal the decision. Let's face it they have a lot of time on their hands. Some unfortunately are successful.

In the last year prior to me leaving we had a few prisoners who had raised complaints about the nurse's fitness to practice. When this happens, this has to be investigated by the Nursing and Midwifery Council, NMC. This is the governing body for all registered nurses who have a PIN number, which is devastating for the poor nurses who are only trying to do their job. They have worked hard to achieve and become registered nurses with the training they have undertaken, and they spend hours away from family and friends working many unsocial hours caring for people some of whom are not grateful and some are clearly evil by making these accusations. It really does affect you when you have tried to provide them with the best care that you can.

The first one in the prison was a complaint raised by a younger prisoner who was trying to get sent out to hospital. It was the late shift, and he had recently been in hospital and received treatment and still had an abdominal wound which he was mainly self-caring for. He had been poking around with it and trying to get it infected again and was not complying with his antibiotics or the wound management plan. He was also being seen by healthcare.

On this particular evening the nurse had been called to his cell as he was demanding to be sent out, he was saying he was in pain and that his wound was infected. She did his observations and gave him some pain relief medication and advised the officers that he was stable and did not require a transfer to hospital. He became very nasty and shouted, swearing at her and yelling displaying threatening behaviour. She was an experienced nurse and had previously worked in an accident and emergency department and was more than capable and experienced to make that judgement and decision. He then complained and a concern was raised regarding her fitness to practice with the NMC. She went through many months of undue worry and stress because of this, and the case was dismissed, but it did not alleviate the stress of those few months that she had to wait for the decision to be made.

The second complaint was directed at two nurses who were called to the overdose I described earlier regarding the man who had been there many years and was known to have mental health issues, and he point blank refused them entry into his cell, threatening to harm them if they went near him. They were unable to get near him to take his observations or to assess him at that point to send him to hospital. He was clearly shouting and fully conscious. His condition deteriorated later, and after they had left to go home, he worsened.

The officers ended up taking him in a taxi when he had practically collapsed and could no longer fight back at them, and he resulted in dying in hospital. The fitness to practice concern was raised this time from the investigation of the death in custody. Again, this caused immense amounts of stress for the nurses and again it was not upheld.

Two years prior to me leaving I had a prisoner who had raised a complaint about me which was dismissed by the trust I worked for and laid to rest, and he was released from prison. He was then recalled, this meant he was not abiding to the restrictions he had been set to follow and he was transferred back into the prison. He then raised a fitness to practice case against me, which was investigated and not upheld, but he then appealed the decision, stating the investigation undertaken by the NMC was not adequate. This has resulted in them having to re investigate.

I have decided to include the report I have had to write and submit to my solicitor who is representing me on behalf of and provided by the Royal College of Nurses RCN, which is essentially the nursing union and professional body offering me support in my NMC Fitness to Practice case. This was raised by the prisoner because he didn't like what I wrote in his notes, and he is trying to sue me for his own monetary gain.

He has also had a court case against the prison attempting to sue them for a claim he has made against the prison for an alleged fall in his cell and that they didn't send him out to hospital.

This claim has not led anywhere and has now been dismissed. I was asked to provide a witness statement and had to attend the court hearing to back up the prison. He was actually released when the court case was held, and he did not turn up for the trial. Why would he? This would have meant him travelling up and paying for his own expenses and effort on his part. When he is escorted to court from prison everything is paid for. Yet I had to take an unpaid leave day in order to attend a court hearing on behalf of the prison which I was not employed by to provide support as a witness and provide background information of his character and the involvement with healthcare. I think I received approximately £30 for my efforts. Where is the justice in that?

Statement for Fitness to Practice

I believe my state of mind to have been clear, focused and stable, I was not under stress at the time of the event. I was calm and clear and made a concise entry in the medical records of **. I stated an observation which I had made whilst following ** across the prison grounds. I had left W Healthcare and saw him in front of me. He was walking with another prisoner, and they were chatting as they walked. The observation was made without him being aware that I was behind him. He appeared to be walking at a normal pace with an unaffected gait. He was not limping or walking with guarded or limited movement. He appeared to be walking normally. This observation was important to make because I was aware that he had another appointment booked at L Healthcare with the doctor regarding his recent 'alleged fall' in his shower, which was unwitnessed in his cell.

The entry was made in his records by myself and at the first opportunity I had, to make the entry. It was written to provide information to other healthcare professionals, in particular the doctors, GPs to provide them with the information which helps in their decision making when deciding upon a management and treatment plan. The more evidence provided gives a more holistic picture when providing care and treatment to ensure it is appropriate to the patient's needs. The more information there is, enables a healthcare clinician to make a fair and balanced judgement.

The statement was a true account of my observation and was made honestly and without malice or prejudice. I was employed, as a Band 7 Healthcare Manager, not only as an Advanced Nurse Practitioner, but also as the Clinical Substance Misuse Manager and Drug Strategy Lead and worked alongside the prison staff liaising with the prison's security department. I was responsible for attending the prison's monthly Security and Drug Strategy meetings, where intelligence reports of prisoners were shared with the relevant department leads including Healthcare. This included those prisoners who were involved in the illicit trading of medications and illicit drugs and those prisoners who were suspected of undertaking these activities. ** was one of these prisoners. I had a responsibility to provide information of suspicious behaviour to the prison and it was within my duty to share this with the Security department.

I had known ** for several years prior to this encounter as he had previously served some of his sentence at HMP ***. He had arrived on a prescription of Methadone, which is a synthetic opiate agonist used to treat heroin or other opioid addiction, and he was known to me as he was one of my Substance Misuse patients and was under my care. I was responsible for prescribing his Methadone treatment and provision of his overall clinical care, including reviews and reduction programmes.

The second time he was recalled to prison to serve a further sentence, he arrived on the prison transport van, and he refused to get off the vehicle and walk off himself. He did not want to serve his sentence at HMP ***. This resulted in him being assisted off the vehicle under restraint also termed 'guided hold' by the prison officers and taken to the Segregation unit. This could have easily been avoided had he not resisted in getting off the transport vehicle.

I was on duty that day and was called by the prison officers to attend the segregation unit to assess ** for injuries he was claiming to have sustained during the restraint. He reported injuries to have been caused by the prison officers due to him refusing to come off the vehicle himself and unaided.

As I recall, he had some bruising and was stating that his neck and shoulder was hurting and requested he have photographic evidence of his injuries. I was not involved in the taking of photographs. The officers would have dealt with this aspect of the procedures. I administered him some simple analgesic mediations to help relieve his pain.

I cannot fully recall all the details of this event and would need access to his medical records to provide further clarity as this was several years ago. I also know that he was a fit man who used to exercise regularly and used to be a boxer, and he participated in organised fights. He would have been used to sustaining injuries regularly during his chosen sport.

Had he have not resisted the officers and come willingly, this event would not have occurred.

Answering the Complaint

I do not dispute the fact that I should not have completed and answered the complaint because it was about me, and it was not appropriate for me to have done so.

The complaint was left on my desk with a post it note by ** who was employed as a Band 7 Healthcare Manager. She started her employment in the role, I believe, in 2021, a few months prior to the complaint. She was not employed as a clinician in this post. This may have contributed to the reason she had assigned the answering of the complaint to me. She was fairly new to the post and was non-clinical.

I questioned her why I had to answer it as it was directly about me and was targeting me. When I attempted to dispute the request to complete and answer the complaint directed at myself, I was advised by ** to complete it because, she said, I was the one who had written in his notes, and knew his history, and had made the observation about him. She also told me she had little previous knowledge of him, or of the event and did not have sufficient experience as she was new to the role and was unfamiliar with how to answer the complaint and the process.

She did not want to listen to my responses or acknowledge my account and experiences which would have enabled her to complete it herself. She felt it should be completed by myself and the post it note she had attached to the complaint had been left on my desk by her, with a note saying, 'this one's for you' or similar words to that effect.

I attempted to dispute ** request and took it to **, another Band 7 Manager and Deputy Head of Healthcare, who had many years of experience in her role in the prison, to discuss and question whether it was appropriate for me to complete it. She agreed I should complete it.

We had a Head of Healthcare in post at the time, employed as a Band 8. He had been on and off with sickness for a substantial amount of time and I cannot recall whether he was at work or absent at this time. During his periods of absence, the work accumulated, and complaints in particular have a time frame in which they must be answered. This may also have contributed to the reason I was asked to complete the complaint about myself.

I was employed as a Band 7 Healthcare Manager incorporating Clinical Substance Misuse Manager, Drug Strategy lead, Advanced Nurse Practitioner and Non-Medical Prescriber within my role. I started on 23/02/2010 and finished in August 2023 having gained 13 years of experience within the prison healthcare system. The first 5 years of my employment, I was employed by Her Majesty's Prison Service. In 2015 the health services were contracted to Northamptonshire Health Foundation Trust (NHFT), National Health Service and I was under TUPE regulations where I continued in my role.

I had experience in answering complaints on numerous occasions regarding medications, dissatisfaction of care and the Healthcare services and was aware of the correct process to follow and the content to provide in answering the initial complaints.

Prior to NHFT taking over as my employer and prior to them having a designated complaints manager in post for the trust, the complaints for the prison would be rotated between the Band 7 managers to answer. As the trust expanded and took over more prisons, we then would be allocated complaints to answer from prisoners residing in other prisons to the ones we worked in to ensure there was no prejudice.

I had to travel to other prisons and recall going into both HMP Onley and HMP Whitemoor to interview the complainant to investigate the complaint and provide a written report for the trust. If a complaint was made about an individual member of staff, it would be investigated by another member of staff and not answered by the individual member of staff, the complaint was about, which was why I questioned that I should not be answering it myself.

** had requested my Nursing Midwifery Council, (NMC) PIN registration number, and wanted me to supply the name of the prison officer who had shared the information that ** had been overheard on the wing telephone asking for a compensation form to be sent in for him. He also wanted me to remove the entry I had made in his medical records.

I answered the requests he had made and did not disclose the information he was asking for, for the following reasons.

1. I did not feel obliged to give any personal details about myself. We had been trained by the prison Security department to never divulge personal information to the prisoners as a safety precaution. Personal information could be shared by them, and passed to their associates, family, friends and contacts outside of the prison and this could put your safety at risk.

2. I could honestly not recall the name of the officer who had shared the information with me, regarding the telephone conversation he had overheard on the prison wing where ** was a resident at that time. ** was overheard requesting a compensation claim form to be sent into him from the call recipient.

It was a long time following the event, that I was asked to supply the prison officers name and don't believe I ever knew what his name was. Officers do not wear name badges to identify themselves to prisoners. This is a security rule to protect them, and they are not under obligation to disclose their names to prisoners if they choose not to. He was familiar to me as he was regularly assigned duty in healthcare around that time, but I do not believe I ever knew his name. There were also approximately over 200 operational staff employed by the prison service, and I did not know many by name.

The officer was working in healthcare on the day he shared the information with me regarding the compensation form. It was a verbal conversation and was triggered when he saw ** in the waiting room of L healthcare, who was waiting to attend an appointment with the doctor on duty that day. The officer felt obliged to disclose the information because he felt it was relevant to ** care and treatment and I wanted to warn the doctor about ** potentially claiming compensation from his alleged fall and injuries he was claiming to have, along with back pain.

I also believed this was relevant information and was the reason I made the entry in his medical notes. I regularly shared intelligence reports with the security department of the prison. Staff were encouraged to complete intelligence reports, and I also regularly received them via email, and specifically about health-related issues, medications and suspicion around illicit trading of medication or drugs.

Part of an officers' role was to provide and share relevant information with healthcare and other departments within the prison, as was mine to document and share in the notes, information which was relevant to other clinicians.

I was employed as the Clinical Substance Misuse Manager and the Integrated Drug Strategy Manager. Prisoners could be manipulative and request stronger/ opiate-based medications for pain which was highly tradeable with other prisoners as it had substantial worth. Medications such as co-codamol were allowed to be kept in their own possession, in their cells.

Stronger pain relief analgesics, such as Tramadol and morphine-based medications were sometimes prescribed but were only administered to patients as a supervised consumption (also known as 'see to take') medication, and were stored as controlled drugs and issued at set times of the day when the healthcare staff were on duty.

These types of medications were sought after as they were difficult to obtain and there was pressure put upon clinicians to provide them by many. Sometimes older or more vulnerable prisoners were bullied and pressured into requesting stronger analgesics by the younger, fitter prisoners, because it is more justifiable and reasonable to prescribe for older patients who suffer from osteoarthritic pain. This type of pain is more often age related. The older patients who it was prescribed for, unfortunately would not get to take their medication because it would be taken off them by the bullies and traded.

I am an Advanced Nurse Practitioner and Non-Medical Prescriber and had been working in the prison environment since 2010. ** had previously been under my care as a patient on the Integrated Drug Treatment System for prisons (IDTS) which was set up in 2010/11 and funded by the government. It was set up by the Department of Health and Social Care to progress the development of enhanced services for prison drug treatment.

** had arrived at the prison on a prescription of methadone due to him having an opiate dependence and addiction. I was suspecting him to have been attempting to obtain opiate based medication for either his own consumption, or to trade for illicit drugs or other items or for both reasons. I do not believe this was an unreasonable feeling to have had and believe it was justified by my experience.

I have worked in several prisons, in addition to HMP***. These include the higher category prisons, HMP Whitemoor, Category A, HMP Bedford and HMP Peterborough, both category B. I was responsible for making decisions regarding the prescribing of methadone to substance misuse patients/ prisoners and where in these establishments, illicit drug use is rife, and security is under much stricter control.

Part of my role was to try and prevent and minimise these incidences from occurring. I refused to remove my entry from his medical records which ** requested I do, because removal of an entry would mean I was falsifying his records. As a registered nurse practising under the NMC code, with reference to recordkeeping, you cannot have an entry deleted. You can request a clinician to add a note to show that you disagree with it.

A patient's record should be complete and accurate to ensure they receive appropriate care. Patients can question the content of their records but not on the basis that it is upsetting or that they disagree with it.

3. I am legally accountable for my actions and can justify my reasons for making the entry in ** medical records. Nurses are expected to keep records of all evidence and decisions and communicate effectively, keeping clear and accurate records and sharing skills, knowledge and experience where appropriate. If an entry needs to be amended because it is inaccurate, the original entry must not be deleted, it must still be readable. NMC Code 2015, updated 2018,

10. Keep clear and accurate records relevant to your practice.

10.3. Complete records accurately and without any falsification, taking immediate and appropriate action if you become aware that someone has not kept to these requirements.

Accusation of Dishonesty and Lying

Failure to remove the entry from his medical records.

I am an honest person and would not falsify facts which are true. I provided information on my observation of ** on that day and with my clinical professional judgement. The prison grounds and prison yard were my description and documentation of where I saw ** when he was crossing from one side of the prison grounds from W healthcare and going towards L healthcare. For clarification and to be more specific, I was walking behind him, and I saw him in front of me, I had not intentionally followed him, along the outside fence of the astroturf football pitch. It was free movement time, when the prisoners walked unescorted through the grounds to reach their destinations. I have not lied or falsified this information.

Some describe the yards as being the exercise areas attached to the prison blocks or wings. When I started at *** there were no exercise yards attached to each wing. The prison grounds were used as the exercise area/yard between the wings. They only built wing exercise areas, often called yards in recent years. I have referred to the prison grounds and prison yard as the same place.

This was all raised again after I had made the decision to leave and I was working my notice and if I had any doubts about leaving, this definitely secured my thoughts that I was doing the right thing.

I knew my time was done and I have no regrets. This sort of thing does nothing for your confidence and really affects you. I feel angry about how it can happen and what sort of rights some of these people have. The justice system seems wrong, and the problem is these people are used to the systems and use it to their personal gain. Without any consideration of the trauma, they have subjected the poor nurse to. I know that I did nothing wrong and was certainly not a risk to the public and feel aggrieved that this has even gone this far.

I will apologise if some of this has read as disjointed. I have never written a book before, and I may never write another. I found that when describing an event or subject it led me straight into another before I had finished the first subject. I just wanted to get all of the information down in detail without forgetting and as so many events happened continuously it is easy to forget some of them in as great a detail as they deserve to be written and described in.

I know people find this subject intriguing and although I have been subjected to abuse both verbally and mentally, I am very grateful that I did not receive any physical abuse whilst inside the prison. I know working there has built me as a person and I have grown stronger and wiser. I have learnt that you must trust in yourself as a person. I have been hurt and felt betrayed at times by trusting too much in others who I thought of as my friends as well as being my colleagues. At the end of the day, I do not take what others say or how they act towards me as a failure on my part or accept the responsibilities of their unkind behaviour as being my fault. I have just learned not to dwell on it and to move onwards, forwards and upwards.

Life is too short to live with regrets. Too many people are ill or are no longer here. So, you have to make the most of it and enjoy it to the fullest that you can. Continue to make memories, with people you can be yourself with, who you love and trust, who remain as your friends no matter what.

So, if you have enjoyed this book, I am happy to have provided some inside information and an overview of the experiences I had during my employment as a prison nurse. I will say there is nothing like it and it suits some people and not others. It is a fantastic learning experience and until I left, I just accepted these strange behaviours and things people do to themselves as part of the norm and the longer you work there the less you question things. You just accept them as they occur.

However, since leaving the prison, I have realised actually how abnormal it is. And that you really don't come across these events in the normal run of life and day to day experiences.

You also remember how patients can actually be very grateful for the care you provide, and they receive and actually that is so refreshing to have again and to feel self-worth. It is refreshing to not have to worry so much about litigation and whether someone is going to report you or try to sue you and that you have to defend yourself against a patient /prisoner because they have a lot of time on their hands and will spend weeks trying to claim some compensation as a source of income from a court case, where you have done nothing wrong. You have to justify your actions and sometimes end up in conflicts with colleagues when you should all be working on the same team.

I now feel revitalised and am loving my new job and practising nursing in another pathway of my career. I left the prison and have moved on in my career from a prison nurse. This time I am working within a GP practice as an Advanced Nurse Practitioner. It was a struggle to begin with as every new job is. I had an intensely steep learning curve to climb initially. I had expanded my qualifications, knowledge and skills whilst working in the prison setting but had only in the majority been caring for and treating men, I now had to expand caring for the general population which includes women and children. This was intense, but I am getting there and will continue to learn and gain in experience. Every day is a learning day.

Whatever type of nurse you are, you never stop learning and there are so many options out there, the diversity is immense. Nursing is an amazing career, and I hope that all of you who are undertaking your training, or those trained but looking for a new path in their career, think about prison nursing. If you think you'd like to take up prison nursing, get in there and try it. It is definitely not for everyone, but I will never regret having done it.

I know I have done the right thing for me, by moving on. I was ready when I left, and it was time. In fact, I waited a bit too long to move but I have no regrets. I loved it and had the privilege to work with amazing colleagues who also became my friends and I appreciate them for being there for me when I needed support, they know who they are.

Also, when you realise you've had enough, get out and move on when you don't enjoy it anymore. I think sometimes you have to hit rock bottom before you can start to build again. You start on a rock-solid foundation. I once saw a poster on a wall, in a substance misuse department which read, 'Make your rock bottom, the foundations of your plan on which to rebuild your life.

The great thing with nursing is you can adapt and take a new path. Don't look back and keep moving forwards.

I truly hope this has given you an insight into what it was like for me and that you enjoyed it.

About the Author

I'm going to write a book I said at work one day, 'what about?' my colleague asked. 'About prison nursing', I have so many stories to tell, experiences you would never dream of and that are so unique in nature, it is beyond bizarre in a normal person's work experience. The role we have as nurses is accepted so readily by most but the versatility and adaptability of us in my work team in the prison goes way ahead all sense of normality. So where do I start? At the beginning? How did I end up in this job?

I didn't start my nursing career until I was 25. I tried various employments and despite my mum being a midwife and having trained as a nurse and telling me numerous times, you'd make a great nurse, I did not consider it as a career until I had discovered other things in life and gained insight into people. She spent her whole career in midwifery working both in hospitals and the community. She also delivered all 3 of my children which is an amazing experience and I'm sure one which does not happen very often in this day and age. She asked me, 'why don't you do nursing? You would make a good nurse, it's a fantastic career,' my response was, 'no, and I'm going to work with horses.'

I left school at the age of sixteen with my seven O level GCSEs, packed my belongings into a horse trailer and set off with one of my school friends to train to be a riding instructor. Between us, we had two mopeds, two horses: feed bins, all of our riding equipment, clothes, living necessities and the horse's equipment. We were quickly to learn the hard way. It was exhausting, we were cold, a lot of the time and it was hard to warm up when you are out in it all day. Our accommodation was a converted corrugated iron garage which leaked when it rained, and water trickled beside the electric plug sockets on the wall. We were so tired at night having to also see to and ride her horses in addition to the four horses and three ponies we were assigned to look after which belonged to the riding school, that we would often eat uncooked food because we couldn't be bothered to wait for it to cook and were desperate to go to bed. This was in the form of frozen fish fingers and peas and pots of ice cream and mousse.

After a couple of months of this, we decided to call it quits and left the yard. She went to a private show jumping yard which agreed to take her with her horses. I moved to a large equestrian centre which was a riding school, took liveries, which are privately owned horses which are looked after by the yard and the services and facilities are paid for by their owners. Some of the horses were also exercised and schooled and trained for the owners. The yard also had young horses that were bought and trained up to be show jumpers and taken out to compete at shows.

I met my friend from London a few weeks after moving there. She had just started and arrived with her own car and posh accent; she was very well spoken. I had grown up in a small country village and gone to the local comprehensive school and had a moped which I used to travel home the forty-mile journey on, once a week and took my washing with me. We were on the government Youth Training Scheme and received £27.50 a week in pay. From this we had to pay £25 a week to the riding school for training fees, accommodation and our food. We also received a grant of £18 a week for living costs. So, we were not on a lot of money, but it taught us to appreciate the value of it. We certainly worked hard for it. My friend was shattered after her first day of hard work. She had learnt to ride at a riding school in London, maybe at Richmond Park, but she had never worked with or owned a horse and had no previous experience of the hard work that it entailed.

I had owned my own horse from the age of fifteen and ridden anything that needed riding including donkeys and even cows and looked after any other ponies and horses I could get my hands on from the age of seven upwards and was very familiar with the work. She was so tired on that day, she had crawled into bed, fully clothed and hadn't eaten. I went to check on her to see if she was alright or needed anything as she was new. We built a solid friendship during the amazing year we spent training together.

 I quickly discovered that my dad was right in that there is no money to be made working with horses unless of course you are the owner of a yard. People do take advantage of your love for horses, and you work such long hours for very little return. I spent eighteen months living away from home at the age of sixteen; I left school and went to work with horses. I trained for the Assistant Instructors and Horsemanship Certificates with the British Horse Society, which I passed and gained the qualifications in. I then returned home and had realised by then that my dad was right; he had advised me to get a proper job and a career. I wasn't really sure what I wanted to do so I applied for and started as an Administrative Officer for the civil service and worked in the local Unemployment Benefit Office (UBO). Dad was happy and I started using my newfound skills at a local riding school where I taught people to ride horses at the weekends.

This stood me in good stead with the public who were from all walks of life and opened up my eyes to the different levels of classes and society. I always opted to go to the voluntary temporary posts when they came up where you went and worked away at other offices to cover short staffing. You also were paid extra for your expenses and the accommodation. I and another girl had great fun staying away from home and going to the bars and clubs mid-week whilst away. I was also lucky to go often to work in London. I stayed with my dear friend who I had met whilst at the stables doing our training together and we went in the evenings together to the outskirts of London to ride her horse. I learnt quickly how to negotiate the busy London underground, which was a revelation once you mastered it and understood it. This was something I have been grateful for; it has been a blessing as I have visited London many times since and never worry about travelling on it.

I was allocated to the Unemployment Benefit office in Camden town, which in the late eighties was pretty rough. There were lots of alcoholics, homeless people, punk rockers, new age, mods, heavy metal, rockers and teddy boys roaming the streets, unemployed and coming in weekly for their giros. There were no plastic screens in their offices to protect the staff when I worked there, but they were installed in my permanent office where it was generally quieter and a lot of people would come in to 'sign on' on a fortnightly basis to declare they had not received any payment for any employment they may have undertaken and to say they were still unemployed and entitled to their giro cheques. We didn't really encounter any trouble or violence in the office but I did learn that the screens, which were there for our protection, also caused communication problems as they made it difficult to hear and therefore people were forced to raise their voices and shout to be heard, which caused frustration and embarrassment for them when they wanted their personal information to be kept private. I found it all to be very exciting when there was any commotion in the office and liked the thrill of a drama.

After two and a half years in the Unemployment Benefit Office, it was merged together with the Job Centre, and we began trying to encourage the unemployed to take up employment and get off 'the dole' by linking them to prospective suitable jobs that came in to be advertised. I also undertook additional part time work in addition to my main post. I worked part time at a local riding school, teaching on the weekends and sometimes the evenings giving lessons, I worked on a temporary basis at a local racecourse on race event nights working on a baked potato stand. I also worked evenings regularly as a waitress in a pub and behind the bar. Another job came in one day from a local auto electrical company. They were advertising for a van delivery driver/ sales representative. I was getting bored at the UBO and Job Centre and thought, this sounds easy enough, I could do this, so I rang them and arranged an interview, explaining that I could drive a horse trailer and small lorry, not really knowing exactly what size van the job would be requiring me to drive.

I knew nothing about auto electrical parts, but it didn't seem to matter. I had a clean driving license, and I could do the deliveries and talk to the customers, in the hope that I could persuade them to buy some of the products. I quickly recognised that being a young female in a 'man's world 'of the automotive trade made me quite popular on the delivery round and I was able to talk. I had never had a problem of being able to articulate, so I got on well, progressed quickly and managed to successfully sell plenty of the products. I remember an incident at school once, my cookery teacher reprimanding me for talking, she said, 'have you ever considered a career in the Navy?' 'No Miss, I answered, why?' 'Because' she answered, 'you would make a bloody good foghorn!' How rude! I thought, but since reading through my school reports, they all reflect that I could have done better if I had talked less and listened and concentrated more. I look at the positive side of this and know that I have very good communication skills and have no problem with talking to people.

Two and a half years later I left the auto electrics company, and with my rucksack packed full, passport in my hand, I left the United Kingdom with my friend I had met through the Young Farmers to go back packing for the next 8 months worldwide. What adventures we had and experiences, but that is another story. On my return, my bosses, true to their word had kept my job for me and let me return, but I had got the travel bug. Soon after returning I left again to go and work on cruise ships for an American cruise line company cruising from Miami to the Bahamas and back for the next eight months. I had a fantastic time, but again, another story.

What I did learn was to mix and have had the pleasure of working alongside people from all walks of life and I gained valuable knowledge in multicultural, multiracial, multinational and multilingual aspects which embedded in me and expanded my personal experiences to stand me in good stead for the future. I experienced the hierarchy within the ships environment from the engineers and cleaners who lived and worked on deck 1, the deck above the engine room. They were the lowest paid and barely saw daylight whilst working and were not permitted to go up onto the decks where the passengers were. At the other end of the spectrum were the highest paid and level, the Italian officers and the captain of the ship and they lived in the very plush cabins on deck thirteen. These were near to The Bridge of the ship, and they had waiter service and lovely balconies on the cabins.

I was employed as a cabin stewardess, a glorified title for a telephone operator, and was responsible for overseeing the Cabin stewards and bell boys. I took orders for room service primarily and manned the phones, we took all the calls from the passengers cabins which aside from food were sometimes for security and sometimes if people were unwell, we called the doctor. there was always a doctor on the ship and two nurses on that ship.

This was probably the first time I had considered taking up nursing as a career. I had thought about it whilst backpacking around Australia, nursing or hairdressing would be required anywhere in the world as they are always needed. Both my parents had moved out to San Francisco for my mum to work as a midwife and be in the sun for a while and get away from the cold of the UK. My older sister had married an American and was living in Colorado Springs and my younger sister had also moved out to Los Angeles and was working as a nanny at the time.

I had noticed that the ship's nurses had their own cabins with portholes in the cabins. They were located on deck four, whilst we were on deck three below and had no daylight. We were cramped into a pretty small space with bunk beds, two to a cabin, but had a shower and bathroom. It really was only for sleeping. I was young, living life, enjoying the weather, partying, scuba diving and generally having a whale of a time.

Whilst on the second cruise ship contract, with a short break in between, I backpacked around Central America and began to think I probably should insider what to do in the long term. I then was twenty-five and still had not decided on a career, so I decided to apply to nursing college. I was accepted and had the relevant qualifications, I passed the application process and interview, and I successfully got offered a place.

The next intake to start was not until the February and I had applied in July having come off the ship. I had no previous experience of nursing patients to and began to doubt myself, 'what if I don't like it? What will, I do then?' So, I thought I' better get stuck in and give it I try before fully committing to three years of training. I applied for and got a job as an auxiliary nurse, as they were called then, now they are called healthcare assistant. I worked on a rehabilitation ward at a large world renown hospital. I did very well, and the next six months passed quickly, so I ready to start my training and had dispelled my fears. I moved away from my home area and settled in Surrey, south of London.

I spent my spare time at my friend's stables, who I had trained with at the equestrian centre. She is still buying and selling horses, riding and training now. I taught some of the lessons but was very lucky as I was able to escort the rides and hacks out at the weekends around Richmond Park, which was beautiful and not like working at all, because I loved it. My student nursing friends joined nursing agencies and were working to earn extra money by providing care in people's homes or working bank shifts on the wards. My extra money was earned doing something I loved. For me, it was a relief from college and helped me out financially. I loved being outdoors with horses, it is in my blood and not hard to work at when you enjoy it so much.

Halfway through the three years of training, I moved back to my home area to move in with my boyfriend, now husband, into our first flat and transferred nursing college continuing my training until I qualified in 1997. I finished my training on the wards of the local general hospital gaining more knowledge, skills and experience to prepare me for being a responsible registered nurse.

My first job as a staff nurse was on a Respiratory Support and Sleep Centre at a specialist cardio thoracic hospital. It was one of few around the country. The hospital was set up originally to treat TB patients. It was an ideally situated place to treat tuberculosis. The patients sat out in individual sheds, like little beach huts which were situated around a duck pond outside in the fresh country air. I soon became part of the busy ward team. We had employed nurses from the Philippines and Spain in batches as part of a big recruitment drive to attract new nurses to the small village, the hospital was located in. It was a lovely place to work, a small hospital with a close-knit community of staff. People often stayed working there for years, some for their whole working careers, it was such a friendly place.

We ran charity fundraising events on a number of occasions which everyone participated in, even one of the consultants who played guitar in a band, helped raise money by performing. We organised a barn dance and fundraising walks to raise money, which we spent on more hospital beds for the ward.

We had several weddings, including mine, births and christenings as well as leaving parties and birthdays to celebrate whilst I was there over the 13 years. I also got married, was pregnant and had my 3 children whilst working there. I will never forget and still keep in touch with many of my nursing colleagues that I had the pleasure of working with whilst I was there.

After having my children, who were settled into primary school, we had moved house, more into the countryside. We bought a lovely farm cottage which had a bit of land and barns, where I could keep my horses and was ideal for my husband to do car repairs and maintenance alongside his day job. I finally began to think about what I was doing with my career. I had been in the same job for the past 13 years. I was in a rut. I had applied for a promotion twice but not been successful.

I had done some courses in nursing, but wasn't really that bothered about doing more studying as you are so busy with young children and family life that you don't have a lot of spare time. I had worked mainly night shifts and weekends whilst the children were small and at school because it fitted in, but I needed a challenge and something new to get my teeth into. I knew I was capable of managing the ward, because I was left in charge, but after not being successful in getting the promotion, I began to look for another job.

This job was to become the next 13 years of my career as a prison nurse!

Printed in Great Britain
by Amazon

56673265R00086